Youth and the Future of the Church

YOUTH
and the FUTURE
of the CHURCH

MINISTRY WITH YOUTH
AND YOUNG ADULTS

by Michael Warren

Gen - 7
21 32
WAR

THE SEABURY PRESS • NEW YORK

1982
The Seabury Press
815 Second Avenue
New York, N.Y. 10017

Printed in the United States of America

Library of Congress Cataloging in Publication Data
Warren, Michael.
Youth and the future of the Church.
Bibliography: p. 146
1. Church work with youth. 2. Church work with young
adults. 3. Youth—Religious life. 4. Young adults—
Religious life. I. Title.
BV4531.2.W38   259'.23   81-16523
ISBN 0-8164-0513-1   AACR2

Acknowledgments:

"Touching the Stories of Young People" and "Evangelization
of Young Adults" first appeared in *New Catholic World*, and
are reprinted by permission.

"When Teenagers Lose the Faith: Phase or Failure" first appeared
in *St. Anthony Messenger Press*, and is reprinted by permission.

The poem "Belle Isle, 1949" is from Philip Levine, *The Names of
the Lost*. Copyright © 1976 by Philip Levine (New York: Atheneum,
1976). Reprinted with the permission of Atheneum Publishers, Inc.

"Live With Me," by Jagger/Richard. Copyright © 1969 ABKCO Music, Inc.
"Under My Thumb," by Jagger/Richard. Copyright © 1966 by ABKCO
Music, Inc.
All rights reserved. Printed by permission.

For Paul Warren,
whose friendship has helped so much.

Contents

Foreword

R eaders will easily see that this is not a book put together
as a unified single statement of youth ministry theory. I
have resisted writing such a book because I suspect that such a way
of exploring youth ministry would tend toward the highly abstract
and would finally not be very helpful. In addition, for many years
now I have feared the danger of overstating the nature of ministry
to youth, making it an entity unto itself, as if it need not be
connected to the emerging future in a young person's life nor to the
wider community and social groupings in which young people
live.

Because of this thinking I have till now been satisfied with taking
an *ad hoc* approach to youth, dealing with questions as they arose
either in my own consciousness or as various persons have asked me
to reflect on particular issues or problems. Such a way of proceeding
has been quite exciting, while at the same time allowing my interests
and curiosity to evolve in a natural, almost leisurely, way.

Since my own deepest interest for many years has been catechesis,
especially adult faith development as it takes place in specific
religious groups and within specific cultures, I have again and again
resolved that a particular statement about youth would be my last.
I wanted to get on to other interests. However, at each juncture
someone would point to an aspect of youth ministry that I had
overlooked or I myself would start, almost without being conscious
of it, noticing another problem. Ironically, then, this book is the fruit
of many decisions to move away from issues of youth ministry.
Indeed, at the present moment, because of the multiple manipula-
tions and pressures afflicting youth in our society, I now recognize

that I am far from having completed my reflection, study, and writing about youth.

Readers will note in the essays certain themes that link much of my thinking. These themes are those of spirituality and culture. The issues are so broad and important that they are at one moment both elusive and open to trivial, inadequate treatment. Of course, culture and spirituality are closely related, and it is that precise connection that makes me want to go much further in dealing with both matters. Perhaps this sense of task will lead me to do a systematic, rather than an *ad hoc,* exploration of spirituality and culture and how they are related to youth. In fact, as I reviewed the contents of the book, I saw that the pieces that meant most to me were the ones that best got at these two issues. In the entire collection the essay most significant to me is the one on politicization; it represents the edge of my thinking and many emerging questions and concerns.

I have been trying of late to persuade persons doing youth ministry to read more—both deeply and widely. There is an extensive literature about youth and youth-related issues. [See Suggestions for Further Reading.—Ed.] To ignore or overlook this literature could mean not only serving youth poorly, but could also imply a disastrous presupposition that the only world is the world of immediate experience. That way of viewing reality overlooks the world mediated by meaning, the world of thought that has been set forth for public discourse and critique. My conviction is that a youth ministry that is poorly informed is open to the most serious errors in dealing with young people, while at the same time being least sensitive to the manipulation, oppression, or trivialization of the period we call youth.

The final three essays deal with aspects of ministry to young adults, that is, young people in their twenties and thirties, with special concern for those who do not have families. Churches in the United States have a tendency to define their ministry too narrowly along family lines and to ignore those persons not fitting into that pattern. Ministry to young adults needs more attention in the future from all the churches.

Introduction

The essays in this book represent an interlocking set of convictions about young people, about the way the churches should deal with them, and ultimately about youth ministry. A network of coherent convictions about some aspect of reality is what we call theory, and in order to introduce readers from many different backgrounds to my own theory of youth ministry, I will explain some of my deepest convictions as well as some specialized terms that I use. These convictions and terms will be elaborated in the coming pages so it is appropriate here simply to introduce them.

Youth Ministry

In some churches "youth ministry" is a euphemism for programs of Christian education. The programs that are called youth ministry, in these churches, are all programs of church education, even if they sometimes include breaks for Cokes and cookies.

However, youth ministry is actually much broader than church education with refreshments. It is an umbrella term to describe systematic attention to a broad range of youth's needs. In my view there are four dimensions to full or balanced ministry to youth, and they are the same four dimensions basic to any fully developed ministry to any age group.

The first is the ministry of the word, which is a ministry that nourishes the meanings or understandings that bind a group of believers together. We could also call it a ministry to the root Christian convictions of a body of believers and to the fact that the group has a tradition of following these convictions. To lose these understandings is to open oneself to misunderstanding. When persons in a group lose their common understandings they have lost a central binding force. As a group their togetherness begins to unravel or come apart. Like our bodies, our understandings have to be nourished, and that is what the ministry of the word seeks to do.

A second dimension of youth ministry is one of worship. This ministry nourishes the response of a person or a group to the dazzling gifts of God. We all need moments of communion with God if we are to deepen our life of faith; and we need moments of celebration in order to stay in touch with God's goodness and to keep naming it.

The ministry of guidance and counsel, including education, is the third dimension of youth ministry. All of us need guidance and counsel from people whom we trust; and we need it regularly, though not incessantly. Young people learn some of the matters most significant to them through guidance and counsel. In addition there are numberless matters not directly related to the meanings that bind a Christian community together but which a person must know in order to grow to full human stature. In fact, there are many young people who are not open to a church's ministry of the word or of worship but who would be very open to its ministry of guidance and counsel. Whereas they might not be looking to the church for religious meaning, they might look to it for other kinds of assistance. The ministry of guidance and counsel can be a place where a local church can meet youth on their own terms and deal with their own perceived needs, in openhanded service.

The fourth dimension of ministry is one of healing, and I add it in order to highlight the importance of attending in a specific way to the brokenness in life.

All four of these dimensions need to be given careful attention if ministry to youth is to be effective. Young people are rightfully suspicious of churches that appear to be concerned only for their "souls." While they themselves might not call such one-sidedness heretical, as I myself do, still they realize that there is something half-baked about one-dimensional youth ministry, and they tend to resist it. They tend to resist those who in the name of the church are hot to teach them things, if they suspect that these persons lack a deep concern for their total life-project.

Youth Catechesis

Throughout this book I use the term "youth catechesis" rather than "religious education" or "Christian education." This preference may be best understood after considering the history of the word catechesis and its relationship to ministry. It is just such an examination that is leading religious education leaders like Dr. John Westerhoff of Duke University to adopt a catechetical language when speaking about Christian education or about religious education within a church context.

Catechesis, and such related words as catechist and catechumenate, are the ancient words used in the early church to name the process by which persons became incorporated into the community of believers. However, after the Reformation the language of catechesis tended to be more favored among Roman Catholics than among most Protestant communities. Recently, some Protestant religious education theorists have been looking favorably on catechesis as a word worth reclaiming and using to describe many of the activities that have been described by the term Christian education. Why are they moving in this direction?

Catechesis is a word that describes all those activities of a community by which both individuals and the ecclesial community itself are led to deeper faith. One can see that such a description goes far beyond the instructional and encompasses, eventually, the way the community itself lives its Christianity. In other words, the ultimate catechetical agent is not any individual teacher but the community itself. Many Christian churches have been striving for years to achieve an integrated sense of the task of Christian education. For example, Presbyterian theorists Lewis Sherrill and C. Ellis Nelson have successfully worked toward such an integrated approach, and what they describe in *The Rise of Christian Education* and *Where Faith Begins* is very close to what is meant by catechesis.

In the early Christian communities, catechesis was actually a lifelong process and not just something for children. As a process it was never completed at any single stage of life, although the mature phase of the process was not in youth but in adulthood. Even more, it was an event that was carefully tied to worship and ritual. Each year the great catechetical event was the Lenten preparation of the new candidates for baptism. The whole community, especially the adults, made the Lenten journey back to their roots, including a memory journey back to their own initiation as believers. The high point of this action-learning was the celebration of Easter, and the baptism of the new candidates at the Easter Eucharist.

One can see here that the catechetical tradition has a strong ritual component, an enactive component, which I find to be especially important for teens. Catechesis is action leading to prayer, and from prayer to further action.

The Christian education of teens, when viewed as catechesis, is clearly not just the religious instruction of young people. Neither can it be carried out by a single person called a teacher. In my experience, young people resist such reductionist approaches to their religious growth. No, catechesis is an activity based in a community. It comes to its proper functioning only when as the ministry of the word it finds its proper place within an ecology of ministry: a balance among word, worship, guidance and counsel, and healing. These convictions are worked out in detail in several of the chapters that follow.

Youth Spirituality

It is possible that every word in this book has been written out of a concern for the spirituality of youth. For me this spirituality is central. I never equate spirituality with the way a person prays. Spirituality refers to the sorts of matters a person thinks are significant in life. In other words, at its broadest level, spirituality has to do with the kind of spirit that is embodied in any person's life. "What is in your heart?" is a most important seminal question about anybody's spirituality.

I consider one of the key issues affecting young people in our time to be the way they are caught within a swirl of agencies, all of which are vying for their attention. All these groups seem to have a message for youth about what is really important in human existence. Some of these are advertising agencies that are trying, often quite successfully, to sell teens not just products or "purchasables," but even more, an entire philosophy of life. We are what we pay attention to. If this statement is as true as I judge it to be, then a key task of ministry to and with teens has to do with the development of a kind of connoisseurship, of a sense of the shoddy and of the worthless, together with a countervailing sense of the beautiful and worthwhile.

In some ways I am suggesting that youth ministry is partly about helping youth to pay attention to the right matters and encouraging in them an appropriately skeptical consciousness about the many con artists who seek to deceive them with junk and fakery. It is easy to run trips for youth, to schedule prayer groups, to sponsor socials. Much more difficult is the task of proposing in a compelling way human and Christian ideals by which to direct their energies for a lifetime.

If this book succeeds in encouraging some persons working with youth in the churches to become themselves more skeptical about the programs offered by many modern agencies and institutions, then the effort that went into writing it will have been worthwhile. I encourage readers to ask relentlessly about any proposal for youth, "Who profits?", if any particular proposal is adopted. I encourage you, my sisters and brothers committed to young people, to help them ask the same question and also to help them speak up and stand up for their own fellow teens. In the church of the future, in the new church, our youth will be invited to stand tall, to have their own say, and to search out their own special mission. Without these young people, with their gifts of energy, questioning, and insight, we will all be severely impoverished. We need the help of our youth if we ourselves are to grow to the full stature of Christ.

1

Youth Ministry in Transition

Among Roman Catholics over the past five years, there have been shifts in the concept and approach to youth ministry that are still dictating significant changes at the local pastoral level.[1] I do not deny that the majority of Catholic parishes have not yet adopted the programs that concretize these shifts in understanding.[2] I suspect part of the reason for this inaction is that the changes involve a more radical understanding of the gospel and call for a revolution in comfortable, business-as-usual arrangements. On the other hand, where a renewed ministry to youth takes root, what develops is an exciting momentum affecting the entire community and showing young people themselves the possibility of engaging in ministry to youth.

Basically, among Catholic parishes in the United States youth ministry has moved away from a period when it involved once-a-week religion classes for teens, sports programs mostly for males, some club activities such as scouting, for boys and girls, and occasional parish dances for teens.

Even in those places where all these activities were in operation, the persons directing them did so in a disjunctive way, with little sense of the need to coordinate with others in other programs so that a unified work for youth would result. The key activity in this arrangement was the weekly session of religious instruction. So long as the young people kept attending, the parish could rest assured that its work with youth was adequate.

But then youth stopped attending. In larger and larger numbers

they stopped attending and at earlier and earlier ages. In the early
'70s particularly, the dropout rate from these programs of instruction
became alarming.[3] Persons responsible for youth work at diocesan
and national levels realized that more and more Catholic parishes
had no youth program for young people not attending Catholic high
schools. In some dioceses conservative estimates said that at least
two-thirds of high school-aged youth were receiving no systematic
religious instruction. In some parishes all attempts to deal with youth
had collapsed. The ministry had dissolved. There were no programs
of any kind for youth. In 1974 the situation seemed to have reached
a low point when it was estimated that two-thirds of Catholic youth
were not being reached in any significant way.

Hidden in this situation, however, were seeds of a new era for
youth ministry. It took time for this new growth to become evident.
Since 1974 youth ministry among Catholics has had a remarkable
resurgence, one indication of which is the increase in articles and
books dealing with ministry to youth.[4] Such writing shows the
growing vitality of this aspect of the church's ministry. These sources
of new growth are what I would like to describe. After sketching
these influences, it will be easier to point out some of the
characteristics of a renewed youth ministry as well as some of the
work still to be done.

There is danger in trying to describe the influences that have led
to any particular development. Lines of influence tend to be rather
subtle and easily distorted. For myself I am impressed with the
influences that catechetical theory has had and continues to have on
ministry to youth. Without suggesting that these are the only
influences on contemporary Catholic youth ministry, I wish to
highlight these influences here because I suspect they are especially
useful in helping us understand what youth ministry is all about.

Catechesis among Roman Catholics has been going through an
intense renewal since the 1930s.[5] One of the landmarks along the
way was the *General Catechetical Directory*, an international
handbook of guidelines published in Rome in 1971.[6] That document
describes catechesis as follows:

> Within the scope of pastoral activity, catechesis is the term to
> be used for that form of ecclesial action which leads both

communities and individual members of the faithful to maturity of faith.

With the aid of catechesis, communities of Christians acquire for themselves a more profound living knowledge of God and of his plan of salvation, which has its center in Christ, the incarnate word of God. They build themselves up by striving to make their faith mature and enlightened, and to share this mature faith with men who desire to possess it. (par. 21)

This passage is important because it puts catechesis into a framework of communal pastoral activity taken by the community in growing ever more faithful to the gospel. This description removes catechesis from the caricature of it found in the question-and-answer catechisms of either Protestant or Catholic origin and ties it to the older tradition of the catechumenate, namely, that gradual ritual process by which persons moved a step at a time to the point where they could name themselves as Christian and enter a community of the faith-filled. Thus catechesis, as pastoral activity of a community, is only partly instructional, only partly implemented by teachers teaching students. Its character is highly celebrative and oriented to activity. As an activity of the community, it involves a lifelong effort at growth through life in that community. Catechesis is not completed at seventeen or seven or seventy. As we shall see, this description has implications for a youth ministry as a comprehensive ministry, rather than as a function carried out in religious instruction classes.

If catechesis is understood as pastoral activity, that is, as ministry, then catechists can be expected to be concerned about the relation of their ministry to other ministries in the church. At the 1971 Roman Catechetical Congress, which in a sense launched the *General Catechetical Directory,* a catechetical leader from India addressed this issue and gave the following analysis of the various ministries within the church, an analysis worth noting because of its significance for understanding youth ministry. D. S. Amalorpavadass of Bangalore outlined what he considered the three basic ministries of the church: the ministry of the word, the ministry of worship, and the ministry of guidance and counsel, including education.[7] To his schema I wish to add "the ministry of healing" and make a brief statement about each of these ministries.

The ministry of the word: This ministry encompasses all those activities by which the church maintains and proclaims the meanings that bind it together. The main activities of the ministry of the word are: (1) evangelization—all those processes that call those outside the circle of faith to stand within the Christian community; (2) catechesis, already described; (3) theology or systematic reflection on the experience of Christian living, including the tradition of that experience; (4) liturgical preaching or breaking the bread of the word in the context of worship.

The ministry of worship: that activity by which a community embodies its understandings and its group life in ritual worship.

The ministry of guidance and counsel, including education: those activities by which a community comforts the troubled and shares its wisdom about the human condition. This is a ministry of liberating the human spirit.

The ministry of healing: those activities by which a community follows Jesus' mandate to free the captives, feed the hungry, bind up the wounded and be a force for justice.

Obviously much could be said about each of these ministries. I wish to advert to aspects of this schema that are significant for youth ministry. First of all, these ministries are not discrete, they are complementary.[8] For example all ministries are ministries of liberation. For a Christian community to embody the word of the gospel, verbal proclamation is not enough. There must be the embodiment of the Good News in deeds of counsel and healing. Worship without concern for the captives and other victims of injustice is foolishness, as Jeremiah warned those flocking to the temple centuries before Jesus. All aspects of ministry converge on one reality: faithfulness to the way of Jesus. This way is to be embodied in a lived community, not just in books or in instructions to youth. To follow this line of reasoning is to see that the problem of youth ministry is not so much one of getting youth to come to church as it is of forming a community of Christians trying to move to ever greater faithfulness to the gospel. This approach to ministry helps us see that any true ministry tends to be comprehensive and to meet persons in their totality.

A second important feature of this schema of ministries is that it places education within ministry, rather than the other way around.

In the Catholic church at least there has been a tendency to take education and reduce it to schooling, but at the same time to make education an overriding and all-encompassing dimension of ministry.[9] Even today, at the U.S. Catholic Conference, for example, the Department of Education is the organizational component that directs the following ministries: adult education, youth ministry, all aspects of catechesis, family life, campus and young adult ministry, and Catholic schools. It also includes what is called the Catholic Biblical Apostolate.

However, some voices are calling for a clarification of categories that will allow education to assume its rightful place as an aspect of ministry and will also allow us to view catechesis as a ministry of the word and other forms of education within the ministry of guidance and counsel. When education assumes its rightful place in youth ministry, the passion to instruct teens seems to find its proper relation to a wide range of youth's needs, one of which is the need to grow in understanding, including the understanding of matters of Christian faith. Ministry to youth, out of this theoretical framework, becomes a ministry to the person in her or his total life and tends to function as a ministry drawing young people into worshiping, healing, guiding communities of persons centered in fidelity to Jesus.

A third key feature of this angle of vision is its way of viewing the catechetical needs of young people. While it does not deny any of these needs related to faith development, this approach does deny that the catechetical needs are always to be given first or exclusive attention. Further, this approach sees the journey to Christian faith as a lifelong journey best understood when seen over the total span of the life cycle, rather than in anxious fixation on the teen years. Not all the serious questions of Christian faith can be addressed before age twenty-one, because not all will be asked before that age. Further, verbal instruction assumes its rightful place as a single medium for sharing meanings that must be enriched by other media: private and group worship and the example of adult Christians striving to live out their commitment to the gospel, walking along with others in doing the deeds of healing.

A fourth feature of renewed youth ministry is not so immediately obvious as the other three. Once we begin to deal with persons in the context of a proper understanding of ministry, we cease to domesticate them by lumping them into the group of the ministered-to.[10] Effective ministry is eventually a call to response. Response to the gospel immediately brings up the matter of the ministry of the ministered-to.

What I have been trying to describe here is not just a community of believers but a ministering community. Once a person enters the circle of that community's inner life, the person herself or himself is called not just to a passive verbal assent to the gospel but to the very tasks of healing, of caring and comforting, of worship, and of growth in understanding that characterize the community. When youth ministry functions out of a ministering community, young people are allowed and encouraged to find their own proper gifts and to develop them for the good of the people. The extent to which the call to ministry is a key component of youth ministry can be seen in the amount of writing dealing with programs of enablement and leadership training.[11]

The following are the characteristics, in summary form, of the renewed ministry to youth that I have described here.

1. Youth ministry is functioning out of a comprehensive understanding of ministry that sees the relationships among various aspects of ministry.

2. Youth ministry has a better nuanced understanding of the nature of catechesis or Christian education. Catechesis is a function of the community and is lifelong. For persons inviting youth into the community, catechesis is but one dimension of their efforts. As such it represents a task that cannot be completed during adolescence.

3. Youth ministry is becoming more and more an active ministry to gifts, calling them forth from youth for the sake of the wider social community and also for the local faith community. Youth ministry is in part a call to ministry.

Someone will at this point say, "But you have not described any actual youth ministry programs." No, and I did not intend to. I hope I have given a way of understanding programs one can find in many different places. There is no single formula for approaching young people and no set of master blueprints. If anything, a sign of creativity is the varied approaches and formats currently being used in working with youth. In the use of weekend formats alone, the variety is very broad. Because youth ministry is becoming more of a ministry *with* youth than one dominantly *to* youth, the natural inventiveness of young people is helping leaders develop flexible initiatives and create fresh programs.

I have been contending that youth ministry among Catholics is in transition from a period when it tended to be fragmented and ill-coordinated, when it centered on religious instruction for those who in one way or another were coerced to attend classes, to a time when it functions as a welcoming posture of an adult community inviting youth to join its fellowship. This transition is still going on. To complete it there are some tasks that need special attention. I would like to comment briefly on five aspects of youth ministry that represent problem areas needing special attention if the transition of youth ministry is to progress.

1. As youth ministry takes seriously the ministry of young people and continues to summon them to their own gifts, the churches can expect more and more young people to come forward asking to be allowed to engage in full-time youth ministry. At St. John's University, where I teach, I have met over a dozen young people looking to be hired as full-time youth ministers in parishes. Five years ago the main outlet of their desire to serve might have been as teachers in Catholic high schools. These women and men have already had various leadership roles with their peers and with younger persons. They wish to move from this experience to some sort of full-time salaried positions. This is a new development needing careful attention if we are not to lose the talents of these persons.

2. Youth ministry needs to pay more attention to youth in trouble. In the churches we run the danger of dealing only with the well-scrubbed, screening out those who in one way or another are especially troubled. If we are to go Jesus' way, we must have special compassion for those at the edges of social groups and those who do not fit in. Youth in trouble include those with family trouble, including runaways and those temporarily needing space away from their families; youth in sexual trouble of various sorts; youth in trouble with the law, especially adjudicated youth who have committed no criminal offense but who are for one reason or another involved with the courts, and often enough, treated as criminal offenders.[12]

3. Much more work needs to be done on programs of education for mature sexuality. Under this heading I include a wide range of possible programs, from programs of sex education for junior-high-aged youth to forums for intelligent discussion of problems related to sexuality.

Other types of educational programs needed include programs of visual education to help young people develop a more critical visual sense and programs of aesthetic education. Should not the churches continue in some ways their traditional role of being preservers and guardians of the aesthetic?

4. More attention to intergenerational components in our youth ministry is needed. A great way to distort the significance of six short years in the life cycle is to become fixated on the problems of those years and then to segregate youth, thirteen to nineteen, from the rest of the human community. Schools are already fostering too much of this age stratification.[13] The churches should be fostering, at least at some times, a more natural coming together in the kind of unity we call fellowship. Youth can easily lose perspective on their lives and get down on themselves. Certainly adult leaders should not compound the problem by isolating youth from the other generations and from the wisdom found in the wider beloved community.

5. Finally, I see a danger in attempting to minister to youth only within highly institutionalized settings. This tendency has been a dominant one for the past several decades in the Catholic church, so much so that now many persons who would wish to minister to youth have no idea how to go about doing so outside institutions. Some persons who come to me for ideas are caught in what I call an "institutional mind-set," which has little sense of outreach and instead demands that the first step always be that of the young person who must present herself or himself to the institution before any attention is paid to personal needs. Much more could be said about this problem, but it must suffice for now to point out that being overinstitutionalized means being highly organized but not *properly* organized. To deinstitutionalize means to pay close attention to organizational matters, but in a flexible mode.

Many of the most significant issues facing youth today cannot be addressed properly by individual church bodies working independently. I have in mind matters that call for significant social change, such as the sorts of legal changes treated by the 1977 Juvenile Delinquency Act, which finally began a process to correct injustices inflicted on youth for decades. There is a need for collaboration in exercising a strong advocacy for youth among the churches. There is also the need to enrich one another's efforts by exchanging angles of vision, strategies, and programs for youth. My hope is that my sharing with you this background of current Catholic ministry to youth will move all our churches one step closer to increased working together and increased sharing of gifts.

2

Youth Ministry:
Search for a Rationale

In the course of discussing the subject with many persons from various Christian denominations, I have been struck by the widely varied understandings of the term "youth ministry." In some places it is used almost as a term-on-paper to cover up the lack of any serious ministry to youth. In other places it is used to describe a concern only for the doctrinal "needs" of young people. I have even seen "youth ministry" used to describe efforts to manipulate or tightly control the behavior of youth. Of course, the term in some churches also expresses broad and well-designed programs to meet a variety of youth's needs, ultimately leading youth themselves to ministry.

As a way of establishing a framework for youth ministry, I would ask myself: What is it I am trying to do with young people? How can I set forth my rationale in as fundamental a way as possible? My hope is that my reflections may shed some light on what the churches ought to be trying to accomplish in their own ministry to and with the young. Thus I must ask myself two basic questions: "Why do I engage in youth ministry at all?" And "How do I go about it, in fundamental terms?" If I can think through to the answers to these questions, then maybe I can shed some light on the matter of Christian education or catechesis of youth.

Why do I engage in youth ministry at all?

In thinking about this question, I have had much help from

17

reading about Christian ministry in missionary countries. In these so-called non-Christian lands there has been an intense reexamination of Christian ministry. Over several decades Christian thinkers in these lands have engaged in fundamental rethinking of what they are doing and why they are doing it. What is important for us is that this rethinking of missionary ministry has had an influence on people in ministry throughout the world, mainly because the churches everywhere find themselves in a missionary situation. This situation has existed for a long time but was not recognized as such until fairly recently. An example of this rethinking occurred at the Second Vatican Council, where bishops from so-called Christian countries of the West found that the situations being described by their brother bishops from other parts of the world were very similar to their own situations back home. A bishop from France, where Christianity is supposedly an ancient legacy, found much insight in a Nigerian bishop's account of his efforts to make the gospel live in his African diocese. As a result, the documents of the Council have a distinct missionary flavor. They have a sense of urgency, a sense that many churchgoers have yet to be converted to Jesus, a sense that the Good News must become good news all over again.

Thus when I ask myself the first question, Why am I engaged in youth ministry at all, I find that my answer is quite close to the rationale currently being proposed for missionaries. What then has been the underlying impetus of my ministry to young people? Has it been to cajole them into joining a club called The Church? Has it been that, if my ministry were successful, these young people would be moved closer to salvation? Have I seen young people as souls-to-be-saved? I must honestly admit that these notions of church, salvation, and souls have not been the vital sources of my ministry to the young. These notions have long seemed to me to be highly abstract and not very compelling as an impetus to ministry. Rather the rationale of ministry comes from a source more personal than these abstractions. That source is the Great Promise of Yahweh fulfilled in the person of Jesus. The rationale as I have been able to think it out for myself goes like this.

The life, death, and resurrection of the Lord Jesus has revealed in a decisive manner the way it is between God and humankind. Each person is the focus of the unspeakable loving-kindness of God. God cherished humankind in an act of pure bountiful love, of naked goodness. As undeserved and freely given, this love is pure gift. When a person understands its reality, this loving-kindness is Good News indeed. Now, Jesus Christ is the most perfect sign of this love of God, manifested as it is in a specific human existence. Jesus gave himself over for his fellow humans and in doing so revealed the possibilities of human existence. Jesus' own existence calls to others to live "his way," to engage in the task of being themselves handed over and of becoming gifts to others.

Those who recognize the call to be like Jesus by living his way are also faced with the Lord Jesus' own command to form a beloved community, which itself is to be a sign of his continuing presence in the world. Members of the beloved community must be what they are, that is, must strive to duplicate in their individual and communal life the loving-kindness of God revealed and made tangible in the person of Jesus. This is their mission. That mission is undertaken, in a sense, independently of the questions of proselytizing. If there exists any criterion of who should deserve their ministry, it is not the criterion of membership in the community; it is rather the criterion of weakness, of abandonment. That is Jesus' way. Those who are neglected, those in extreme need, those who are outcasts are to be given special attention, although there will always be a call to be servants to one another within the community.

The invitation to join the beloved community is a secondary question, though not for that reason an unimportant one. The witness of a life centered on the way of Jesus will itself be a powerful call, a powerful message of Good News. Their personal and communal authenticity is itself Good News or kerygma, giving power and credibility to the verbal announcement of the gospel. In other words we never bring the gift of service to others, we never bring the gift of our love to others without also bringing the gift of the source of that love. That is why Paul exhorts the early community to be prepared always to give an account of their faith, that is, of the font of their behavior, which witnesses to the mystery behind the Christian life. We can hope to hand over in an explicit way our love for Christ to those we serve. But even if that hope is not realized, we are still called to love them the way the Lord Jesus showed us. In the lives of the saints as in the gospels, openhanded service to the stranger is especially prized. Since the stranger is not of one's own group and has no status in society, generosity to such a person mirrors the indiscriminate and free love of God.

Such then is one person's rationale for Christian ministry. You will note its emphasis is first on being in touch with the shocking message given in the person of Jesus and with a lived commitment to his way. This rationale presupposes that faith lives in the lives of individuals and communities and not in books. Faith can be elaborated, explained, and systematized in books, but it shouts, it dances, it lives and takes flesh in people. Finally, this rationale depends on these individuals and communities to be ready to give an account of their own lived experience of faith. What I have been saying here is similar to what a missionary in India wrote about evangelization a few years ago:

> Evangelization is not a mere theoretical teaching about Christ, an apologetical argument about Christianity, but a sharing of the Christian experience, a testimony to the transforming interpersonal relationship brought about between man and God, and among men by and in Jesus Christ. To tell another what one has seen, heard, touched, and experienced is called bearing witness. That is what Christ asked of those men who had experienced him. "You will be my witnesses not only in Jerusalem, but throughout Judea and Samaria, and indeed to the ends of the earth."[14]

Now it seems to me that what I have said here is a mouthful. It is miles from the approach of some local churches to youth, namely, that of running programs for kids because the parish council or church board has mandated that something be done. If a youth ministry were to adopt a rationale similar to this one, some things would immediately have to be done differently. There might have to be more prayer and reflection on the part of the adults. There might also be more concern for the faith development of the entire community, not just of the young people. Youth on the margins or youth who do not fit might receive more attention. Liturgy would have to take a more privileged place in the church's life. Whatever decisions must be made, one thing will be clear. Ministry is not an appendage to one's life, like Little League or scouting. It comes not from an encounter with appeals from the pulpit for new teachers but rather from encounter with the person of Jesus, sometimes in moments of silence, sometimes in moments of joy, and many times in moments of pain.

How do I go about ministry?

What do I do, once I realize that the gospel and my personal gifts and the needs of the community call me to do something? There are two fundamental ways of going about any ministry. I would like to reflect upon each in as basic a way as I know.

The first approach to ministry was brought home to me powerfully by the following quote from William F. Lynch's little book, *Images of Faith:*

> . . . I think that if there is any one consistent theme in my own examination of the life of the imagination over the years it is this: that imagination, if it is to get anywhere in insight, understanding, or vision, must progressively move through the finite, the detailed, the definitions of the phases, the time, the stages of the human and of human life. Faith must make the same patient movement.[15]

To this passage I would add: "So must ministry." Let me repeat what Lynch writes, substituting the word "ministry" for Lynch's word "imagination":

> . . . I think that if there is any one consistent theme in my own examination of the life of ministry over the years it is this: that ministry, if it is to get anywhere in insight, in understanding, or vision, must progressively move through the finite, the detailed, the definitions of the phases, the time, the stages of the human and of human life. Faith must make the same patient movement.

We can quickly see the ramifications of Lynch's insight for ministry. There is no idealized ministry. Ministry involves entering the lives of the persons being ministered to. Those lives are very specific and concrete, formed by intimate relationships, by education and jobs, by geographical environments and cultural influences. The minister must in a sense be born again, come alive all over again to these persons in this environment. A minister can put real flesh on the bare bones of a desire to serve only by becoming incarnated among the people he or she wishes to serve. The gospels portray Jesus as putting flesh on his last supper exhortation to his disciples by washing their feet and by breaking bread with them, and then by going through death so they might live.

Ministry in practice is far from an abstraction. I must enter the lives of these specific people. I, the specific person I am, with my limitations and my gifts, must do so. I must have an eye for these people and an ear for them and a heart for them. If I could ask ministers any *one* question to find out if they were engaged in true ministry or merely in wishful thinking, I would ask them to tell of the deepest hopes, the deepest hurts, the worst self-deceptions, the most cherished joys, and the unrealized potentials of those people they are supposedly serving. If any minister knew, and could speak of those matters in the people's own language and images, then I would suspect that this minister had become flesh among this people. When people ask me where they should start in youth ministry, I usually advise them as follows: Get to know some young people. Get to know their gifts and possibilities. Call them to be better than they presently are. These same persons will lead you to the next step in your work.

For me the most encouraging aspect of contemporary youth ministry is a recognition that young people have needs other than doctrinal ones. Research such as that found in Merton Strommen's *Five Cries of Youth* is helping us recognize that we must minister to persons as integral beings—and not merely to aspects of persons. In order to take seriously the faith-development needs of young people, we must also take seriously a broad range of their other developmental needs. When young people realize that the church is concerned about them as a whole and not just about their disembodied souls, they begin to respond. It is not a matter of doing a good "con" job, of playing our cards right so that we can get them to do their religion homework; I am intending an integrated concern for people, including the religious dimension of their lives.

Some would like to minister to the young by proclamation (a kind of proclamation quite different from the announcement of the Good

News) and by fiat. The possibility of proceeding this way with young people is long past. The only way to minister to the young is to move among them, listen deeply to what they are saying, establish bonds of caring with them, work along with them. Only then can one begin to speak the truth credibly among them and only then can one begin leading them deep into the mystery of Jesus. The reason so many Christian education or catechetical programs for young people fail—or worse yet, become a laughing-stock to the young themselves—is that many adults are ready to "teach them religion"; few are willing to enter their lives with the kind of patient walking along with them that Jesus exemplified in his own ministry.

Entering the lives of youth is not something that demands length of time so much as quality of presence. The presence needed is an adult presence, willing to speak the truth, even the painful truth, but always with compassion. There is no such thing as a supercilious compassion. Compassion is not born of superiority. Compassion springs rather from a recognition of a common humanity, of a common bond that bridges even the gulf of many years. The same catechetical leader from India quoted earlier expressed the matter this way:

> . . . we Christians feel our human solidarity with other men. We share one goal, that of development and ever greater communion with one another, the quest for God and a discovery of Him. We experience the same joys and sorrows, the same problems and anxieties as our fellow men. But as Christians we experience the joy and peace that come from hope, the hope that our present fellowship with God in men will one day find its perfect fulfillment.[16]

If we reflect on those who have influenced us in our own growth and development, we will most likely find some key persons who cared for us, who saw our possibilities, and who encouraged us to recognize these possibilities ourselves. We will also find that our growth in faith has been aided by those who shared with us some of their own journey to faith, which is my next topic.

The second fundamental way we go about ministry to youth is by sharing with them our own experience of the gospel. Let me illustrate what I mean. In India, when a missionary wishes to preach the gospel to a Hindu, he may likely be asked the question: "Tell me of your personal experience of God. Speak to me of your communion with this God." If the missionary cannot claim such an experience, much less share it with him, the Hindu may laugh at the presumptuousness of one who wishes to speak of a God one has not encountered in silence and awe.

I believe that in our contemporary missionary situation in the United States many young people and many adults have an attitude similar to that of the Hindu. They are looking to those who exercise a formal ministry to give a credible account of their own experience of the Father of Jesus. They are looking for women and men of interiority, who are in touch with their own experience of communion with God. We have all had the experience of being deeply moved when a person of spiritual depth shared with us some of his or her own spiritual life. That sharing finds echoes in our own lives, sometimes helping us discover long-hidden longings for communion with God. On the other hand, we have also experienced the numbing effect of a sermon full of words but empty of any meaning. We feel numb; we feel cheated; we feel that something that should be made new has been made old; beauty has been disguised and draped in rags. I wish to recall what our missionary in India said about ministry's not being a mere theoretical teaching about Christ or an apologetical argument about Christianity but rather a sharing of the Christian experience. Our ministry is meant to be a testimony to the transforming interpersonal relationship brought about between a person and God and among men and women in Jesus Christ. It involves telling another what one has seen, heard, touched, and experienced.

Some people may be discouraged at being reminded that ministry involves being in touch with their own experience of God and a willingness to make that experience available to others. They will say that they cannot sustain that sort of sharing for long. They are right. It is not always appropriate or possible to share one's depths with others. But what is important for all of us is the conviction that ministry involves the pursuit of holiness and communion with God. At some level, ministry involves being a "holy person" in the Hindu sense (which is quite close to the traditional Christian sense.) It means that we ourselves are engaged in a continual search for God in our own existence. When that is the background of the minister, then catechetical work or Christian education with young people has a chance of success. With that background, the catechist or Christian educator will not be handing on someone else's faith but the Christian tradition as it has made a difference in one's own life.

3

Touching the Stories
of Young People

O ne of the chief gifts adults who intervene in the lives of youth have to give them is the gift of language. An adult who would intervene with young people in a helping or a healing way must somehow enable the young person to speak of his or her own life in a significant way. How? By all the natural ways: by having a posture of welcome toward the other, by a careful and patient process of paying attention, by an inner attitude of truthful compassion that sees where the young person is struggling to grow.

I have asked many adults over the past several years to describe those older persons from their youth whom they remember with the most affection. Invariably they single out those who listened to them, who heard them out. They were the adults who took time to hear their story and to help them recognize both a pattern and a hope to these stories. Rarely does one meet a person who was listened to attentively and deeply, who claims that such an experience of being heard did not help. In fact, just the opposite is true. People tend to remember with deep abiding gratitude these experiences of having been attended to. They attest to the healing power of human presence and understanding.

One of the chief gifts adults who intervene in a *religious* way in the lives of youth have to give them is the gift of *religious* language, one aspect of which is to encourage the young person to speak of his or her life in its religious dimension. Rahner states that to lead a person to the stage of an explicit faith always involves assisting the understanding of what has been already experienced in the depths of human reality, so that it can be more clearly seen in its character as grace or gift. It is out of such a context of human experience that "the multiplicity of propositions formulated for belief . . . give a much clearer impression of being something people could make something of, rather than a mere exercise of formal obedience to propositions. . . ." (*Sacramentum Mundi*, II, 311).

The following presentation represents an attempt to speak in a more or less formal way to young people about their own life story. Those who have responded best to the approach attempted here are those around age sixteen or older. Besides addressing the proper age group, one has to create a context for these ideas to be heard and then digested. Ideally, some group building would precede such a presentation, which would in turn be followed by a period of silent reflection and journal-writing. A final step would involve small group discussion and prayer/liturgical ritual.

Readers will note that the presentation itself attempts to stay close to the concrete and the specific, making much use of images, anecdotes, and examples. The second part of the presentation is far more abstract than the first, since my expectation is that as persons become engaged in a process of deep reflection on their own lives, they are ready for reflection in a more abstract mode.

Other explanations are needed to contextualize properly the following presentation. These are given after the presentation's conclusion.

Understanding Our Own Stories

I'd like to share with you a letter I received recently from a sixteen-year-old girl in New York whom I have known for about two years. In a way it shocked me but it also helped me to understand something very important not only about her but about myself and about lots of other people. Let me read you her letter. She told me I could as long as it would help someone. All I have done is change her name to Janet.

Sunday Night

Dear Mike,
    I'm sending you another of "those" letters but right now I feel so bad that I just can't see what I should do. Last night I had

another big fight with my mom and as usual it was over nothing. And then everybody else in the family seemed to get involved— all on the side against me.

I can't stand this place. I know it's another one of my awful statements but I've been thinking about it ever since before I began my homework and after I finished it. I just want to avoid everyone here. The trouble is you can't do it forever; someday I'll have to see or talk to them, but how long will it last? I wish I were older and could leave this place but I can't. I'm stuck and it's rotten. I just want to cut myself off from everyone here. God, I'm so confused.

Last night seems so trivial yet I know it will happen again. Nobody seems to care about me or my feelings.

I didn't go to church today cuz I would've had to go with them and I couldn't. I just couldn't sit with them. Don't you see? It would've been one big joke. Maybe it's contradictory, but I see that they are here and I'm trying to believe they care but like I said when I saw you they are just parents, not friends. I don't even know for sure that I want them as friends.

I hope this situation isn't going to continue forever. I feel so bad and I don't want to feel that way. I mean I feel as if I am bad and ugly. I don't want to feel so ugly inside but I do anyway.

Please write and let me know what you think. Am I going to feel like this forever? I'm scared.

Love, Janet

Wow! At least that was my reaction. What is your reaction? Is Janet's letter typical or untypical? What was her problem as she wrote the letter?

As I said, this letter helped me understand some things about people in general. One of them is that we all are in danger of seeing the world through the end of a bean blower. Know what wide angle binoculars are like? All binoculars restrict vision, but wide-angle ones give a wider view. Well, a bean blower gives the narrowest possible field of vision. You see practically nothing. Or it is like looking at a mosaic. Once I visited the tomb of Mother Cabrini in New York. I entered the church by the side door and knelt before the altar under which was a wax figure of Mother Cabrini. You could walk around the rear of the altar near the rear wall of the church. That wall looked very strange to me. It was filled with little stones of different colors. Nothing seemed to match. It was clear that a lot of work had gone into that wall but it looked ridiculous—until I was in the back of the church and could see a magnificent mosaic of scenes from Mother Cabrini's life. Mosaics don't make sense right up close. They must be viewed from a distance, with perspective.

Janet's letter reminded me all over again that life doesn't make much sense when it is seen with your nose against it, without any perspective. That is a lesson we all have to learn over and over again. I had to learn it when I was a senior in high school. For most of that year, my height was five feet seven. I still don't like to admit that or even talk about it. It brings back to me again how hard it was for me at that time being five feet seven. I didn't like being that height. I didn't like *myself* at five feet seven! I wanted to be taller. I was angry about the whole situation. It was frustrating wanting to be taller and knowing that there wasn't a single thing you could do about it but stand there in your socks and be five feet seven. So I compensated; I developed a big mouth which often got me a fat lip. Even when the doctor told me that year that I was growing rapidly and would probably be about six feet tall, I just couldn't see it. I didn't believe him. But sure enough I grew almost five inches that year. It was like a miracle and to this day I'm glad I'm not five feet seven (Frank Sinatra, Sammy Davis, Jr., Joel Grey, and Robert Redford notwithstanding).

All of us are a story. It is not that we have a story. We are an on-going story. When we forget this, our life becomes a series of unconnected events, connected only in the sense that they all happened *to us*. But when each of us gets a sense of our own history, there is a whole different quality to the events of our lives. Things that happen to us cease to be just "stupid," and they become instead filled with possibilities, because we have a sense that we have come from somewhere and are going somewhere in life. We find a sense of direction.

It is not just a matter of remembering our story, but of how we remember it. Let me show you what I mean. Think for a few minutes about your own story. Imagine that all through your life so far someone has secretly been making home movies of your every action and every thought. You weren't aware of it but it is all on film and you are the star. You've been on candid camera the whole time. From the first moment of birth, this film takes in much more than a picture of you in the buff on a bear rug. It has everything, through age two and then on through age five and all the incidents of your life through age ten and then through age twelve, right through last summer and this fall up to and including last weekend, last night, and today. So it is on film. So what? Well, let's imagine that there's going to be a showing of your film, and everybody is invited—all your closest friends, including the friend you have cared most about; your brothers and sisters will be there too and your parents and your aunts and uncles, including the ones you like best and those you can't stand. Friends of the family and friendly neighbors are all coming. All your teachers of course will attend and your grandparents. They are all there in the room; they are excited, gathered around you to see your life. The lights go out and the film rolls.

How would you feel if that scene were to be real, if such a movie really would be shown? What would it be like for you to sit there as one of the spectators? Every time I have asked that question I have gotten the same answer.

Almost all say they would be ashamed out of their minds at their own "this is your life." Do you know why? Because they don't really understand their own story. They think their story is centered around all the embarrassing things of their past, around their failures and uglinesses. But that is only part of the story. Let's go back and watch the story. Don't just look at the diapers you wore as a baby. Take a look at how much joy you gave to your parents. Look at how loving you were. You probably were like most children—a real hugger. Look at the little homemade Christmas gifts you gave your parents. Listen as the film rolls to the comments of your parents as they watch: "I remember how thrilled I was the day he or she did or said that." Look at the little acts of care you did for others that they might have overlooked but here on the film are seen by everyone. Is it possible or would you ever consider the possibility that at the end of the film everyone would clap for the special person you are? Picture the scene: The clapping; your friends picking you off the floor and trying to revive you. Well, most of us don't think of that when we first hear about our hidden movie, our personal candid camera. *And the important thing is that we will never remember or want to remember our story*—our past story—unless we recognize that there is a lot of goodness in it, a lot of our best selves. (When Janet wrote me her letter she had forgotten about her goodness.)

Let me use another example. (Hold up a large white sheet with a small black dot in the middle.) What do you see? What do you see on this sheet?

Did you see the 99 percent of the area that is white? Did you see the whiteness or did you just see the black dot? There is a lot more to this sheet than one black mark. In fact that is the most minor part of it. But because we do not want it there or because it is different from the rest, we focus only on that. That's pretty similar to the way we can look at ourselves and our stories. We see only the black spots; we don't let ourselves see the rest of the picture. And yet most of us probably are aware that we often love the quirks, the black spots, in others. For example: The students in my class at the University were standing around one day talking about Maria, the quiet little coed with lots of freckles. The conversation turned to how much Maria hated her freckles and thought they were ugly. The girls talked about what you could do to cover up freckles. Jim was there—very tall, handsome, articulate, and bright, a debater. Quietly and very seriously, Jim said, "I love freckles!" Everybody got embarrassed and felt awkward, including me. What we didn't know was that Jim had started going out with Maria. See, he loves Maria *and* her freckles, or maybe Maria in her freckles.

Now we all have to do some work. We have to do some remembering. I want to ask some questions to help all of us remember our own stories. Let's try to discover our stories. (We often invent stories, but our own personal stories we never invent; we only discover them and then, I would hope, come to love them.)

Let's start with the people in our stories. Our stories are *made*, not so much by events and happenings but by people.

People

• Who are the people we fight with most? (Oftentimes we find out who is really important in our lives by discovering whom we care so much about that we fight with.)

- Who is the one, after fighting with whom you feel the worst heartache?
- If you had to pick three persons in your life that you absolutely could not think of not knowing, i.e., these persons are so important you had to know them to be who you are, who would they be?
- Out of those three if you had to pick the one you needed most, who would that be?
- If you could go back in your life and find and be with a single person from your past whom you never see anymore, who would that person be? (That person has been important!)
- What death in your life has pained you most? (The more that death hurt, the more you know that that person is in a sense still very much part of you, still lives in you in a sense.)
- Who are the ones you would have been better off not knowing, the ones who have had a bad influence on you or who bring out the worst in you?
- Who is the person who stirs the greatest feeling in you?
- Who is the person who most challenges you to be better than you are, who is calling you to develop your gifts most, maybe even to the point of annoyance?

Places

- What place on this earth has been for you the most beautiful, the place whose beauty touches you most?
- What place outside your home do you go to when you want to be alone and at peace and thoughtful? How often have you been there?
- If you had to go back in your mind and remember at the age of five the place in your home where you felt the greatest warmth and peace, where would that place be?

Events

- What choices have you made so far in your life that have made a real *difference?*

• What choices have sent you down a particular road rather than some other road? (Remember that sometimes choices are made by not-choosing, by drifting, by being afraid of choices. You can't *not choose*.)

• If you had to list them, what have been your three greatest joys so far in life?

• What have been your three greatest sorrows or disappointments?

If you had to say thank you for *one* thing in your life, what would it be? Now, one more question—in some ways the most important for the rest of the things I want to say. Can you honestly say that God has not been present in those people, places, and events of your life? Does it seem to you that God has been leading you in some mysterious way, hard to see but also hard to not see? Have you thanked God recently for any of the beautiful people in your life, even those who no longer live or those you no longer see? When was the last time you thanked God for the beautiful places? (Some would say that warmest place in their home when they were five was also the place where they got their first sense of the warmth of God's love.) Have you forgotten those secret times and places known only to yourself and God when you experienced his presence powerfully? Were you seven or ten or twelve or fifteen?

Our Future Story

What have we been considering in our past and present stories? Knowing and remembering our story prepares us for the most important part of it, the part that is still hidden from us, the part that is to be, our future story. In a way it is hard to think about it, but for a few minutes we have to think about it. I have a couple of things to say about it. In a way our future is already with us. It can be found in our dreams. Our daydreams tend to be about our future; our night dreams tend to be about our present and our past. So we daydream about the ideal person we would love and about the persons, places, and events of our future that will make us most happy (or sometimes most unhappy). We also daydream through worry about what we fear most in our future.

Now nobody knows the future, and nobody knows the future less than I do. But I can suggest some things about the way we think about the future. First, most of the horrible "what if" dreams we have don't turn out the way we dreamed of them. Horrible things happen to all of us, but they tend to be complete surprises. The "what if" dreams either don't happen or don't happen in the way we worried about them happening. It takes time to realize this. There is great truth in the old saying: "Yesterday is gone; forget it. Tomorrow never comes; don't worry about it; today is here, get busy." For myself, at times I have to take my worries about the future to the Lord and put them in his hands, trusting that he really is leading me somewhere. But, see, we will never do that until we appreciate how much God's care has already happened in our past story. If we haven't thought about it as a story, then we can't appreciate or get a sense of the full scope of God's action in our lives.

A second thing about the future. It is promised to us. God has promised to continue to care for us. That doesn't mean that things will always turn out the way *we want*. We all already know that about life. Even so, God will still continue to care for us.

But there is more about the promise of the future. We ourselves are a promise. We are part of God's promise to someone else. God is waiting to care for someone, possibly many, *in us*. We may not have met them yet. Some of them have not yet been born. Some can be born only through us—in many different senses. We are called to be a promise to many. We are called to be a gift—note, not to give gifts but to be a gift—in our own selves. Don't you see how knowing our story helps us face that fact too? That means that at five feet seven or whatever, with black spots or freckles, we, the special people we are and have become, are being called to smile on the part of our story still to come—the best part.

Realizing that our future is calling all of us forward as person-promises to others helps us understand the incompleteness of our stories. Patience with the future is often a problem for people. Some want everything to happen today, or, at the very latest, tomorrow morning. They don't seem to be able to wait and let things take their course. These people are like the child who bakes bread for the first time. The child smells the bread baking, and because it smells good, he or she wants to take it out of the oven immediately. Any experienced bread-maker knows that to take the bread out as soon as it smells good and starts one's mouth watering would be to ruin it. It cannot be taken out until it is done. You have to wait until it is done; it is no good half-baked.

A high school student I know in New York City showed recently a keen understanding of the kind of patience with the future I am speaking about. Her parents were worried about the sex education classes she was taking in her public school; at least they were until the other day when she came home and explained to them an important realization that came to her during those classes. She realized, she said, that she is physically mature, fully mature enough in her body to have a baby. She also realized that the physical mothering is only one small part of being a mother. She said she thought that the other capacities needed for being a mother—emotional maturity, intellectual development, capacity for care, her personality—all need a good bit more development before she will be ready. This girl shows real wisdom about her life-project, part of which is patience with her own growth and development.

The final thing I have to say is about how knowing our own stories helps us understand the stories of others. Whenever we love someone we want to know that person's story. When we know someone's story it is a key step in being able to love that person. It allows other persons to become new to us. Knowing and loving our own story is not boring. When we get in touch with it, it certainly does not seem stale. Instead it becomes new. We can always come to understand new aspects of it. The same is true of other persons' stories. Knowing their stories is often the clue to allowing them to be original and special to us.

To me it is important in meeting other people, even strangers, to realize that they have a story, most of which is hidden from me. Keeping this in mind will help us not take people for granted. Take, for example, the sports star who seems like a stuck-up grouch. There is a story to his behavior. Knowing that the story exists might make him more understandable and thus even more standable. We have to remind ourselves that other persons are a mystery to us, with many beautiful and many sad things in them hidden from our view. When we remind ourselves that there is much we don't know about other people, we tend to become more respectful of them, because we tend to be careful with things (and persons) we don't fully understand.

Sometimes I think that the last step in growing up comes in being able to think about our parents' story—their full story. I suspect that some adults who seem very grown-up have not yet made that final step with regard to their parents. Imagine asking some of the questions I asked earlier, first about your father, then about your mother. They have had joys and heartaches and fears, just like us. They too have loved and been loved by many people. They too continue to be a promise and a gift. Often they are a promise and a gift to us, but we are not a promise or a gift to them.

Maybe after finishing this chapter you might want to search for a motto that would summarize for you your life story up to now. Think about it for a couple of days and try to discover the motto that best expresses where you are headed. I know older persons who have mottoes like: The bread is rising, or I've only just begun; or, Come, Lord Jesus, or Lord, show me where you live. Make up any motto you want. Just let it represent your smiling on the best part of your story, what is to come.

Reflection Points

1. I prepared the original presentation for young people after reading statistics about the escalating suicide rate among teens and those in their early twenties. I sought to give some sense of hope to young people coping with all the strains of growing up. I believe, however, that words or ideas such as those contained in this presentation will remain empty without the on-going presence of some persons who clearly care, and, ideally, of a community. Such persons will be a sign to the young person that his or her life project is worth the effort. The more I study about young people and work with them, the larger looms the importance of adult models, mentors, gurus, persons however described, who become points of orientation for youth.

2. One of the key matters young people need to understand is touched only vaguely at the end of the presentation. This is the matter of how their own personal story intersects with the stories of others and, more importantly, with societal stories, that is, with the

story of the people, the nation, the race. Because those dimensions of story do not appear here does not mean they are not of special importance. One session does not a program make. A person can be trapped in his or her own privatized, narcissistic story if it is not complemented by other dimensions that get at humankind's larger story. One of these dimensions is that of the religious tradition; others are those of nation and international community, and ultimately those concerned with the species. What is alluded to at the end of the presentation is the family story, an issue that can show a young person that his or her life moves into the past beyond the self, and, one hopes, into the future beyond the self.

3. Although I originally prepared this presentation for youth, I found that adults have responded to an adapted version of it even better than the young people did. In every case my presentation to adults was in the context of a series of reflection sessions on adult spirituality. Apparently many adults do not get much opportunity to see the connection among the various components of their lives and find the uncovering of these connections a process that gives added coherence to their lives.

4

When Teenagers Lose the Faith: *Phase* or *Failure*

Several years ago, while working in Washington, D.C., I resolved never again to speak with parents about the faith development of their teenage children without at the same time speaking with the teens themselves about the faith development of their parents. How did I come to such a decision? The following scenario explains it all.

The adult audience was breathing down my neck like a house dick on a shoplifter. They barraged me with questions.

• "Our sixteen-year-old girl goes to church with us each week, but she is inattentive and seems bored. When I talk to her about it she just shrugs it off as unimportant. What can I do about it?"

• "I told my son that if he didn't go to church on Sunday he couldn't stay in our home; he's eighteen and I don't want his atheism to rub off on our younger kids."

• "We gave our children twelve years of religious education and now that they are in college three of them have dropped out of the church. Where did we go wrong?"

• "My twelve-year-old doesn't want to go to Sunday school. He says it's a drag. What can I do to get him interested in religion?"

• "I think the teachers and the new way of teaching religion are responsible for our kids losing their faith."

Such questions and comments came at me like so many bony-fingered jabs in the ribs. I was, to say the least, uncomfortable.

We were in the second week of a five-session adult education series—"Understanding the Development of Teens"—and the procedure was not going the way I had planned. A lecture-discussion program, the series dealt with the whole range of developmental tasks of adolescence, examining within that framework teens' religious and moral development. My aim was to put the adults in touch with some of the information available through developmental studies—but also to make them aware of what they already knew about their own development and that of their daughters and sons. Part of my approach involved using excerpts from letters I had received from young people over the years and from other kinds of autobiographical accounts of what it is like to be a teen. It was a good program design. I knew; I had run it before.

But alas, with this particular group the approach was not working. We weren't getting anywhere. My purpose was to give some perspective on adolescent development—the long view. However, bypassing my input, the group chose to focus on specific behavior of young people. At least they did until the McNultys spoke up. In their sixties, silver-haired and distinguished looking, the McNultys were now grandparents. Marie McNulty began to speak of the religious journeys of their four children. She explained that the one who seemed to be most stable and untroubled about religious questions during the teen years underwent a religious crisis in her early thirties that finally led her to the serious study of theology. Mrs. McNulty went on to speak of her anxiety over one of her sons who continues to be a church dropout. "At first I felt alienated from him and resented what I considered to be his irreligion. Then one day I realized that his total way of living is better than that of some people who are frantic churchgoers. I had been looking at Sunday church attendance as the only religious behavior but came to see it was only part. Every day now I deliberately remind myself that my children remain in God's hands."

John McNulty also spoke, but in a softer voice and to a stronger hush. "What about us, what about Marie and me and our religious development? Sometimes I think that I am just beginning to understand what it means to be a Christian. I don't pray now the way I used to. It's different, maybe because I'm different. I know in my own life I've had more than one conversion so far and may have more. Maybe our kids will too."

That said it. For several more minutes, the McNultys kept on speaking. They had the floor and the rapt attention of all of us, whose minds had swung from anxiety about the religious problems of teens to the broader question of our own lifelong religious growth. I breathed a sigh of relief. We were back on the track. The McNultys, with the wisdom of experience, had led us to the perspective I had hoped the research would lead to.

Since that time I have been convinced that the best way of helping parents understand the religious growth of teens is to place that growth clearly in the perspective of lifelong religious development. If we do not start from this end of the question, then we can be misled into thinking that the most important faith crises occur before age seventeen or that teens question their faith but that adults do not.

Therefore, when I am asked to help parents understand the faith-growth of their daughters and sons, I usually begin by asking the parents what they think the next step is in their own faith development. The question of the "next step" in one's response to God can be asked of persons of any age, from the thirteen-year-old to the eighty-three-year-old. Anyone who can hear and tolerate that question can also discover the answer for him or herself. Occasionally, when I pose the "next step" question, parents will stop me and explain, sometimes calmly, that they did not come to talk about the eighty-three-year-old but about the thirteen-year-old. It is then that I try to explain that all the research I have seen on the religious development of teens insists that the single most important factor in predicting the later faith practice of young people is the faith practice of their parents, particularly of their mothers. For some parents this is not an easy truth. It is easier to put one's hopes for religious growth in Sunday school classes or Catholic high school religion programs or to blame the persons running such programs, than to face the possibility that, as a parent, the key may well be one's own faith.

The nature of the process of communicating Christian faith is such that the question of teen faith development is intimately tied to the way adults hold their faith, and even beyond that, to the way whole parish communities live their faith. Many of us adults know from friends of our own age that halts or blockages in one's religious development occur as much during the middle years as during the early ones. In fact, figures published six years ago by the National Opinion Research Center pointed out that the largest percentage of Catholic dropouts from regular Sunday worship occurred among persons over fifty-five.

After working with adults in Washington and New York for the past ten years, I myself am convinced that the most serious problem with religious development is a sort of mid-life numbness of spirit, a closing-off of religious questions that is actually the atheism of the religiously half-awake. As concerned as I have been for young people, my greater ache is for adults tied in knots by a kind of consumer-lust always alert for the next thing they will buy, persons bent on having an ever greater slice of the United Statesian good life, even at the expense (literally) of one's brothers and sisters.

Someone will say, You are helping me understand the complexity of the problem but you are not helping me understand what I as a parent can do to help my own children grow in Christian faith. In hopes of giving some specific suggestions, I offer the following guidelines that might be helpful to parents and others dealing with teens.

1. *Keep in mind that religious development is like all other development.* We can sometimes assume that religious development somehow occurs outside time and is unaffected by all the factors that affect other aspects of personal development. A good analogy for religious development is physical development; very few persons are impatient with physical development. They know it takes time and that one must crawl before one can walk. Full physical development takes years. In fact, most parents rejoice in the very gradualness of it. They have the trophies of their children's incremental progress: the first tooth, a photo of the first step, a bronzed first shoe, a lock from the first haircut. Physical development is dramatically visible; other aspects of development are more hidden but also more continuous since they are open to lifelong progress. A person's intellectual, emotional, and psychological development can, indeed must, if it is not to decline, continue through the life cycle, though not in an unbroken upward curve.

The same is true of religious development. Like all other

development, it is characterized by progress and regress. There are limbo periods or periods of latency during which a person seems to be bogged down and marking time. Such periods seem to be important especially during transitions, when one is moving from one phase of development into another and needs lots of psychic space before plunging ahead. Also, there are times when a person is in two different stages at once. A friend of mine calls this the "mugwump posture," with one's mug on one side of the fence and one's "wump" on the other. On a fence is an uncomfortable place to be but sometimes a necessary place.

For example, at some point in life, a young person has to move from what Roger Balducelli calls a "socially induced faith" to a faith of personal commitment. Such a move involves a transition from one position to another. Like switching apartments or homes, a personal transitional move takes time and some amount of personal energy. Let us consider a fifteen-year-old who has grown up in a particular Christian family. She or he has had a consciousness throughout life of being Christian, a fact that was largely taken for granted. My last name is such and such; my address is such and such; my religion is Christian. However, somewhere along the way, the person comes to realize that what was assumed as being the way things are and have to be is, in fact, a choice and one that he or she is going to have to make. At this point the person is ready to move from socially induced faith to a more adult faith of personal commitment.

In *Love or Constraint*, his book on religious development, the late French psychiatrist Marc Oraison tells a story of special power about a young man of a devout French family, who shocked his parents by announcing at age seventeen that he had "lost" his faith. Knowing his depth of reflectiveness, his parents, hurt though they were, decided to respect his decision. It took eight years of patient waiting before their son came to them and told them that he had recently been converted to Christian faith. The words of this young man to his parents impress me greatly: "I can tell you now that if you had not shown the respect for my liberty of judgment that you did, I don't know if I should have ever found the Faith again."[17]

The point of the story is not that all young people will make the dramatic return to a church that this young man did. In fact the story itself is not so much about a young man as about his parents. My hope in retelling it is that parents may remember the fact of life that religious development is a lifelong matter and is best understood in the perspective of an entire lifetime.

2. *Maintain your own religious commitment and pursue your own religious development as yours.* The problem of religious development is not a technological one and is not solved by across-the-board application of scientific formulas. We in the United States are famous for making things work, but sometimes we inappropriately apply mechanical systems to persons. There is a sense in which any one person is powerless to demand a religious commitment from another person. Such a response must come from within the other person's human freedom and decision to hand one's life over to God. That kind of personal decision can be assisted only indirectly by persons who know how to be present to other persons in humanly, including religiously, significant ways. In the face of this creative powerlessness over another's faith response, I would encourage parents to focus more seriously on their own religious growth, because that growth could ultimately be the most powerful sign to youth of the beauty of Christian faith.

Writing in *New Catholic World,* Rosemary Haughton expressed this matter well.

> I sometimes think we get the business of family religion upside down. There is, naturally enough, so much emphasis on the children—their needs, their problems, their future—that we easily feel that the whole spiritual life of the parents exists in order to bring up the children as Christians. We don't say this, or even consciously think it, but we behave as if we did. Parents often adopt customs such as family prayer, for instance, because they feel it is good for the children, *not* because it seems to them a proper expression of their own need to worship, or as nourishment for their own Christian life.
>
> That can be a good thing. Many parents have begun to do, for the sake of their children, things they hadn't seriously considered before, and discovered in these things great benefit for themselves. All the same it is, in a sense, the wrong way around, for a real family spirituality is like the culture of a nation—it is only solid and enduring when it is part of the whole atmosphere of daily living, not something taught to the children to improve their minds (or souls).

Maybe married couples should think about this more in the early days, but whenever they do begin thinking, it really is important not to let religion seem something the grownups do for the sake of the kids.[18]

Fostering their own religious growth is what enables parents—indeed, any adults—to be with young people in religiously significant ways. In my judgment, knowing how to be with youth in religiously significant ways is perhaps the most crucial knowledge for anyone who would hope to invite them more deeply into the mystery revealed in Jesus.

Fostering one's own religious development should be an important step toward influencing the religious development of teens. Here I would add a reminder about the relationship between influence and care. I have often asked myself which is more important to me: influence or care. The ministry of the catechist or youth worker has always seemed to me to be basically a ministry of care; but on the other hand, I have always wanted to influence young people toward ever greater horizons in their own lives. Would I sacrifice one for the other, influence for care or care for influence? For a long time I was not sure of my own answer to this question. Then one day I came to see that what I wanted most in my personal dealings with young people is the very special kind of influence that comes only from a clearly perceived care. Influence *and* care are related matters. If I as a nonparent concerned for youth cannot forget that relationship, then parents themselves must not. If I had to choose between the two, I would choose care, as a source of special influence in the lives of youth.

3. *Pay attention to the quality of lived faith in the parish community.* Christianity is a faith rooted in community. Jesus summoned his followers to join the beloved community, and it was the experience of the Spirit of the Risen Jesus in the midst of his beloved community that bound the faithful together in the primitive church. The sign above all signs of the beloved community was the sign of love for one's fellow persons. Young people today continue to need that sign of love if a parish community is to be a credible sign of the presence of Jesus. When congregations become communities

of the faith-filled, then they will provide young people with believable living exemplars of the Good News.

If I were a parent I would be vitally concerned that my parish community had trustworthy guides for my own children and for all the young people in the parish. All of us are looking for trustworthy guides to aid us in our journey to faith. There is a certain amount of directing that goes with being a guide, but a trustworthy guide to adult faith has a specially delicate task of directing. This person points out general directions and then gives the supportive presence that encourages people to find their own way on their faith journey. When I have questioned them about their faith development, hundreds of adults have attested to the key role played in their growth by a trustworthy guide.

In speaking of a trustworthy guide, I am not referring to just any teacher but rather to a catechist who has a certain quality of life and wisdom. In fact, a coach, chaperone, a youth worker—anybody—could function in such a role. There is more to finding such persons in a parish than making panicky late-August pulpit pleas for Christian education teachers. Trustworthy guides have become such through a life of active reflection. They know and show Jesus' Way because they go the Way.

Are not parents trustworthy guides? Of course. That is the very heart of parenting, and ultimately other persons in our lives are perceived to be so in reference to the primal trustworthy ones, our parents. However, again and again I have seen teens need or at least profit by the beneficent presence of others who are quasi-parent figures. I think of them as uncle and aunt figures, because the relationship they have to young people seems so powerful and of such lasting influence. Sometimes teens need trustworthy nonparent adults in whom they can confide. Ironically, far from luring youth out of the family circle, they aid young people to go back to the family with increased perspective. The matter is obvious to those many parents who have been aunt and uncle figures to children of other parents. My point is that parish communities need to be more conscious of the key role of such persons.

A final but important note about the parish community. I would encourage parents to pay more attention to the quality of worship in their parishes. In worship the community embodies its faith stance. A German theologian, Josef Jungmann, once wrote that down through the ages whenever the church wanted to teach a truth, she established a feast. What sometimes appears to be a crisis of faith can in fact be a crisis of worship.

Conclusion

For some years now I have felt that a person could not intervene well in the faith life of a young person, say, someone of fifteen, unless the adult had the imagination needed to think of that young person at twenty-five or forty-five or even eighty-five. To be able to think in such a way is to put teenage faith-growth in the perspective of lifelong religious development. Persons of limited perspective who deal with youth are dangerous. It is difficult enough for young people to have perspective at their age without adults compounding that lack. A trustworthy guide knows distances and reminds one to enjoy the going, the journey, and not just the arriving. The journey must be taken one step at a time. A true guide understands gradualness.

The other perspective I have suggested for parents is that of the parish community. As important as families are, they must be put in perspective with other communities to which we all belong. A key one is the wider faith community especially at the parish level. Sometimes in speaking with parents anxious about a teenager's faith development, I have seen that they are actually unsure if their youngster will grow well in the parish and its business-as-usual inattention to the gospel.

Probably the whole matter of lifelong faith development can best be understood in the context of gifts. The search for Christian faith of youth is actually a gift to adults, if only they are willing to receive it. Youth will force adults to reexamine assumptions and to rethink old positions. In the early church it was the catechumens who called the community to renewed faith as much as it was the community who called the catechumens to a new faith. On the other hand, adults are called to recognize that they themselves, in their own persons as developing Christians, are gifts to young people searching for Christian faith. The place above all where we all gather to celebrate the gift of the Spirit of Jesus and to look into one another's eyes is at the altar, where we share the gifts of nourishment. May it ever be so.

5

Approaches to Youth Ministry

Over the past several years, as I have traveled throughout the United States as an advocate of the holistic approach to youth called youth ministry, I have been astonished at the varied presuppositions there were about what youth ministry is and how it should be done. Not too many years ago in one denomination, these varied presuppositions surfaced as an open dispute among the members of a key national-level board set up to advise the church on policies related to youth. One faction insisted that the board's focus should be on noneducational and noncatechetical activities such as scouting, sports programs, competitive marching bands, and the like; another group insisted the focus should be more toward developing those aspects of the lives of youth that were not being attended to by other agencies: developing youth leadership and youth service such as peer ministry; programs to assist the sexual development of youth; and special attention to their spiritual development.

In my own experience of working with local churches in youth ministry, I find a more graphic example of differing presuppositions. The youth-ministry team I worked with, serving eight churches in New York City, had contacted a certain pastor in the hope of setting up a weekend of Christian living for the older youth in his church. The pastor expressed interest in our idea, but was quick to point out that his young people already were involved in a weekend program and did not have time for another. He proceeded to describe the details of his weekend program. It involved a twice-yearly trip to a dude ranch in a state park area. The young people went horseback-riding, swimming, hiking, and so forth. The name of the dude ranch, interestingly enough, was The Eternal Ponderosa. It was located on Schroon Lake.

To the pastor this weekend was just the sort young people both wanted and needed. To me it sounded, on the one hand, funny in a ridiculous way and, on the other, boring. I found out later that the youth who attended claimed these weekends would have been very boring except for certain extracurricular activities they had contrived for themselves in an effort to keep excitement high. Not all the activities at Schroon Lake were humanly enriching ones. What our team had in mind for these young people was somewhat different: a coming together for a weekend of serious grappling with life issues and an examination of the feasibility of the Christian way for contemporary youth, both undertaken in a rich atmosphere of care and celebration. When eventually we had our weekend of Christian living with the youth in that church, they found it to be both exciting and enriching in a way The Eternal Ponderosa was not.

Because so many persons working with youth seem to operate out of differing presuppositions, I have tried to examine various approaches to youth ministry to see if they can be grouped into basic categories and analyzed. The process of classifying activities according to some schema is the process of creating a taxonomy, a sort of diagram to show how one kind of activity both differs from and is related to another. For the purposes of analysis and description I will classify three different basic approaches to youth as three different "models" of youth ministry. My hope is that we may all have a better sense of what we are trying to accomplish and a better appreciation of the efforts of others which may be in a different direction from our own. Out of such appreciation may come other attempts to expand our vision and improve our efforts in youth ministry.

Three Basic Approaches to Youth Ministry

Currently in the United States, there are three basic approaches to youth ministry: the approach that emphasizes contact; the approach that emphasizes content; and an approach not much in evidence but gradually emerging, the communion approach. After stating the goal of each model, I will examine each approach in four aspects: (1) the attitudes of the adults in each approach, (2) the kinds of roles the adults in these programs assume, (3) the kinds of programs in each approach, and (4) the contribution of this approach to young people.

As a final point, I will make a critical analysis of each approach as an attempt to do youth ministry.

Approach I: Focus on Contact

The goal statement of this approach appears to be: We must keep our young people in touch with the church. This goal statement is kept alive by the attitudes of the adults favoring this approach. If we could imagine ourselves sitting in on a local church board or vestry or parish council meeting, we might hear these attitudes expressed this way.

A man stands, well-dressed and appearing to be from one of the professions, and says, "We don't want to lose our teens. We know that young people undergo a crisis of faith in their teens. As a result they drop out of the church. And it is no wonder. Our church has no programs for them. They don't feel welcome here. We seem to have programs for every group except the teens. No wonder they stop attending on Sunday."

A woman stands and explains that as a mother of two teens and two teens-to-be, she is also concerned. "There are many bad influences on kids today. Their hangouts are not always the healthiest. We all know that hangout over on _____ Street, where cars spin rubber in and out of the parking lot all night long. My children tell me that the younger set congregate in the playground behind the junior high school on weekend nights to drink and God knows what other carryings-on . . . We need programs that will keep them off the street and out of the way of some of these harmful influences. They need healthy programs in healthy places surrounded by healthy faces."

As the discussion continues other convictions are expressed, such as, "We want them to know our church cares. We want them to know *they* belong to the church too." "We need more friendly faces for them in our church. After all if kids get into trouble, the kind of trouble parents don't get told about, where will they turn for help if they can't turn to the church?"

Such attitudes all express concern for prevention and for welcome. These adults want to prevent the alienation of the young from the local Christian community. They want to maintain the affiliation of youth with the church. Otherwise, when they are older, this reasoning goes, the young people will become permanent dropouts. However, the attitudes move beyond prevention to welcome. They want youth to have a place and to feel thoroughly at home in the local church.

Contact Programs

The programs that grow out of these adult concerns are many and take different names in different churches. Usually there is a variety of sports programs, often covering seasonal sports over an entire year. Some of these are first-rate, providing excellent competition and the young people are proud of their accomplishments in them. In some places, though not as commonly as one might hope, sports programs are provided for both sexes, with equal attention to sports activities for girls. All of them involve the use of church facilities, such as gyms or sports fields. They also provide hours of contact between young people and dedicated adults from the local church.

In addition to sports, there are various club programs, such as scouting—boy/girl explorers, sea scouts, or Campfire Girls. In rural areas there are 4H chapters. In effect these are secular programs offered under church auspices. There are also dances, sometimes on a regularly scheduled basis, bringing together young men and women in a socially healthy atmosphere, free of drugs or alcohol. Conscientious chaperones willingly devote many hours of their time helping plan these dances, being present at them and later coordinating the cleanup. There may also be social or cultural trips, though these seem to be not as common as other programs. Under this category fall ski trips, camping trips, trips to the theater or sporting events. (Even a weekend at a dude ranch could provide a healthy recreational event for teens.)

Adult roles and contributions

In the contact approach adults assume roles of chaperones,

coaches, planners, persons-who-care, advisors, and even occasionally of counselors. The contribution of these contact programs is multiple. The programs provide opportunities for fostering in young people a "sound mind in a sound body," an ancient and solid approach to youth. They also help achieve the goal of helping teens stay busy and out of trouble. A more significant contribution comes through the adult roles mentioned above: advisor and counselor. It would be interesting to question all adults in the United States who work with youth in these kinds of church-related programs; to ask how often they find themselves giving private advice or counsel or encouragement to young people. We might find out that coaches and chaperones are engaged in a much more significant intervention in the lives of youth than some of us realize.

Another aspect of these roles is that in many local churches one can find remarkable adults willing to accept contact roles but who clearly do not want to assume any sort of formal teaching role. Unfortunately, because often they are not able or willing to be teachers, their potential gifts in dealing with youth are overlooked. In my opinion the special significance of these kinds of programs can be found in the attitude of welcome and friendliness the young people find in those running them. Teens are in painful need of being welcomed, especially by the church. The significance of those who do the ministry of welcome with teens is not to be minimized.

Approach II: Focus on Content

The goal statement of this approach is: We must communicate to our young people a solid understanding of the church's beliefs. If we were to continue our imaginary church or parish council session, except at a different church, expressing a different set of concerns, we might hear someone stand and say, "We want them to know their faith. It is important to have contact with the church, but it is the kind of contact that I am concerned about. I want them to have contact with our doctrines and our truths." Someone else adds, "We want them to grow up in their faith as Christians in our church. We don't just want them to know things. We want them to live their faith. We want them to live good clean lives, and beyond that, to grow in their love of God." Another person picks up this theme. "We need to provide opportunities for them to worship, too. They will never understand worship if we don't have good liturgies or good services for them. They need to use their own music at special worship programs just for teens, at least sometimes. If they don't, they will probably get bored and drop out."

These attitudes are basically ones of concern to communicate correct understandings and concern for the eventual development of practicing or "churched" adults. These adults wish to pass on to young people maximum understanding and maximum opportunities for the development of a relationship with God.

Content Programs

The chief kind of program that emerges from the above convictions is a Christian education program aimed at giving sound doctrinal instruction. Such a program often uses the best and latest texts available and also employs good audiovisual materials. Attention is given to the proper selection of curriculum suited to age levels and stages of development. Sometimes the volunteer teachers in such programs attend several training sessions each year to sharpen their instructional skills, or deepen their own doctrinal understanding.

In some churches there are "rap" group sessions for older teens who refuse to attend classroom sessions. These small-group, rather loosely structured discussions are often held in homes; sometimes the group will study one topic for a specific number of weeks before going on to another topic. The topics are often selected by the group according to their own interests. Thus a group could spend three weeks discussing friendship in the New Testament before going on to sessions on sexuality or on cults, and so forth.

Small-group and large-group worship for teens is another kind of program that could evolve from the content approach. Young people have a role in planning and executing these worship programs, especially in selecting and playing their own music. Sometimes the young people have their own liturgical or worship committee, on which adults will serve in advisory roles.

Adult roles and contributions

These are programs where adults serve as religion teachers or instructors. They also function as discussion leaders or facilitators.

The latter are skilled in understanding group content and in helping to continue a discussion from week to week. They also tend to be comfortable with teens in informal settings. Such adults may also play the role of organizer and fellow planner, as in worship committees. They may function as friend, advisor, and counselor, though such roles are more likely to evolve in more informal programs and in longer periods spent with teens.

The value of the content approach is that it provides opportunities for growth in understanding church teaching and for clearing up misunderstandings about what the church's teaching on a particular matter actually is. Further, this approach offers opportunities for good communal worship. Finally there is the sign of adults who care enough for their own doctrinal understandings to want to share them with others.

Approach III: Focus on Communion

The goal statement of this approach is: Let us welcome young people into communion in the Spirit of Jesus manifesting himself in this community and in their own lives.

As the adult attitudes emerge at a council or vestry meeting they sound like this:

We want to set up opportunities in which we can share with young people both the history of this community's faith in the Person of Jesus and our own local history of growing in that faith. We want to initiate them into the secret of Jesus-faith. We will function as their guides in helping them become familiar with landmarks on the journey to faith. We have a sense of the way, because we ourselves are on the journey. We wish our young people to walk along with us.

We want to set up occasions where a community can pray, worship at the table, and play together. We want to move to being a fellowship, with our young people invited to assume their own proper place at the table as our fellow sisters and brothers. We want to hear their own personal word of faith in the Lord—or their own struggle toward that word—because that word or that struggle is a gift to us, enriching us. We need their gift, especially their own special insight into the meaning of Jesus for this body of his followers.

We wish to be a community of care, concerned for the total development of our younger sisters and brothers, but also calling them to be part of the community of care. We want to invite our young people to join us in searching out the poor and the weak and the wounded to whom we offer care and encouragement.

We invite young people to discover, eventually, their own special gift of ministry. We shall be at their service in helping them recognize and prize their unique gifts. Our community needs to be enriched by their searching, their own special insights, and ministry.

Communion Programs

As the reader might already suspect, these programs are basically the same ones that nourish the adult community, the very community into which the young people are being invited. Specifically these programs would include the following: Opportunities for significant faith-sharing between fellow Christians, such as weekends of reflection on the gospel; days of learning and sharing on topics of current interest to the community, such as specific social justice issues; seasonal programs for group study and sharing, especially during the times of Lent and Advent; on-going programs of care for the poor or service to those in trouble. There might also be activities centered more specifically on prayer, worship, and play; prayer groups; family programs of study, worship, and fellowship; other opportunities for small-group worship tied to specific occasions, such as a wedding. In addition, a community would have occasional programs geared specifically to the needs and interests of young people. Here, education for sexual maturity is an example. Outreach programs for youth in trouble would be another.

The chief program in a communion approach would be the weekly celebration of the life, death, and resurrection of Jesus by the community gathered at the table.

Adult roles and contributions

The adult roles in this approach are obvious. They are all roles that stress friendship and mentorship, while working out of the kind of equality called fellowship. These are the roles of friend, of discerner and affirmer of gifts, of catechist and mystagogue, and of fellow searcher and fellow Christian. The special value of the communion approach is in offering adult models of living faith, encouragement to grow in a total human way in the beloved community, and the gift of summoning one another to ministry. Another way of stating the contribution of the communion approach: the life of the community is the chief instructive element. The life of the community *is* the program; special projects for youth are ancillary to that core.

Critique

The final section of this analysis must be given over to a critique of each approach, in terms of what is lacking in each. The *contact* approach's main problem is that it does not go far enough. It tends to treat young people as disenspirited bodies. Adults share their time, facilities, and so forth with young people, but tend not to share their faith with them. Possibly some adults fret about the problems of integrity in sharing one's personal faith, which the sharer knows is still incomplete, on its way, or in process. Many have a fear of seeming phony. Yet it may be more phony to share our time and energy with youth and never disclose the source of our motivation. A special danger of a contact-only approach is that it sees the church as a kind of private social club, like the Rotary. Here we have the community of believers at its most superficial. It is like a mother feeding her children on a diet of cake.

The main problem with the *content* approach lies in its lack of a true concern for young people. It tends to treat young people as disembodied spirits. Many youth seem to be saying to the churches, "Don't be concerned about my soul unless you are concerned about me, the whole me." The content-only approach tends to deal with teens as assimilators of doctrine, ignoring the broader scope of their needs. In fact, if I had to choose between the contact-only or the content-only approach, I would choose the first, because it shows concern for a wider range of youth's needs beyond their doctrinal needs. Ironically, preoccupation with doctrinal needs to the exclusion of other aspects of a person's life seems against the spirit of the gospel. The content approach, as a one-dimensional approach to teens, is like a mother feeding her children a steady diet of raw meat.

When originally working out this taxonomy, I intended to criticize the *communion* approach, but when I got to that point in my study, I saw that it was a balanced, nuanced approach in every respect. It includes the best features of the contact and the content approaches. One objection against it could be that it is idealistic. It is well to remember, however, that sound practice comes from having appropriate ideas carefully turned into correct action. Poor practice often comes from inadequate ideas being put into practice. Youth ministry needs the right ideal translated into practice. We have to choose among the ideals we wish to follow and then decide if we are willing to work to achieve them. Here I am saying that the communion ideal is the correct one and can be realized in practice.

The communion approach is like a mother feeding her children a balanced meal at the family table all together in joy. A student once amplified this image by saying that it is more like a farm family, having all had a part in the planting and harvesting and cooking of a meal to which they all sit down, taking joy in one another's contribution. My hope is that this analysis of approaches to youth ministry may convince us to invite youth to bring their own gifts and stand with us at the table of the Lord as our sisters and brothers.

6

Spirituality for Teens: *Finding the Right Direction*

So many people come at spirituality for teens from so many different angles, with so many different presuppositions about it and about its nature, that it is sometimes difficult to know if we are all concerned with the same reality. Therefore I have chosen the title and theme of finding the proper direction in teen spirituality, first in thinking about it and secondly in actually assisting teens in their spiritual growth. So at the beginning I want to comment on how we think about spirituality; and then, later, to make suggestions about directing young people in their own spirituality. I would caution the reader that these thoughts are themselves in process and need to be clarified, amplified, or even corrected.

How Do We Think About Spirituality?

Let me give two scenarios, dealing with two actual persons I encountered recently.

The first is of a young woman of thirty-two, describing how she fought off a particular attack of depression by "fighting with the Lord." She is a follower of a form of Christian spirituality that looks for specific signs of God's immediate activity. She had driven from Long Island to New Jersey to visit her former boyfriend/lover/ companion, and found, after a long, tiring trip in the rain, that he was not home. She drove back home in a state of depression. This was her account of what happened.

> I was fighting with the Lord. I was having a great fight with him. I was telling him off and asking him why he did all these bad things to me. I was really mad at him. And it was raining, and you know how it is with me when it's raining; it's a real bummer. But then, I'm driving along and fighting with the Lord, asking him for a sign that he is still taking care of me, and suddenly on the car radio came one of those missionary programs, you know, about people who are for the Lord and trying to bring others to the Lord. But then just as I started listening to this program, the sun came out. It was the end of a long, lousy, rainy day, and the sun was out. The Lord was telling me that he was still my friend, that he was still my Man.

The second scenario is of a twenty-one-year-old student, in his last year of college, who is holding two jobs and doing lots of serious fudging on his schoolwork. We talked about his nonperformance in a theology course entitled "Marriage in the Lord":

> Listen, you keep talking to me about education and learning and all that ____. I'm not into all that stuff. I have two jobs right now to pay for my tuition, and all I want is to get that damn degree, and I really don't care about all those things you keep saying are important. You talk about "being reflective" and "the project of becoming more human." Man, what I want is my degree, to get a good job and a good salary, because next year I want to get married. I want to get married and make some money and get somewhere. Me and my girl, we want to buy a house, but we're not going to live in it all year round. We intend to play. See, we ski and that's big for us and it isn't cheap. Someday I'm going to have me a Mercedes, and man, I really don't know how much of your reflection and "human project" garbage (no offense) I'm going to need to drive that set of wheels.

Two scenarios, seemingly different. What do they have to do with spirituality? Both of these persons represent spiritualities, though we often don't think of such attitudes as spiritualities, especially not the second. When originally I had these conversations, I thought they were at opposite ends of the pole, but on reflection they are more close to one another than apart. Both are manipulating life, one through hard work, the other through an almost magical view of her relationship with God. Both, then, represent spiritualities, and I am not sure that either of them is a Christian spirituality.

My point is—and it is the first of three introductory assumptions about spirituality that could clarify the way we think about it and approach it—my point is that a human being cannot *not* have a spirituality. Man is spirit, and embodies in her/his life a range of values, of hopes. Every human person has a stance toward life, and even if that stance is one of active not-caring then *that* is what the person stands for. That stance is a spirituality. A human person, then, is in a sense what she or he longs for, what she or he values, and what she or he hopes for. Our choices are not accidental aspects of our lives. Choices actually define us and shape the kind of human spirit, of human project we are.

I consider it a mistake to think that spirituality is a matter exclusively of prayer and worship. These are important matters in any religiously oriented spirituality, including any Christian spirituality; but spirituality itself, in its widest meaning and seen from its widest angle, is the entire way we approach life. In this widest sense of the term, then, spirituality deals with *where we are coming from*. The reason so many attempts to deal with the spirituality of adults and teens fail is that we do not deal with where people are coming from. So in this wide sense, there is no question whether or not a person will have a spirituality. The question is not *whether;* the question is *which,* which spirituality is worthy of a human being? Although I say it is impossible not to have a spirituality, I judge it is very possible for a person to have a desperately poor spirituality, or an un-Christian one, or a quasi-Christian one.

A central question for persons concerned for youth is: what kind of intervention should Christians make in the lives of one another, and especially in the lives of young people, to foster an appropriate embodiment of the human spirit?

In dealing with the question I do not intend to deal only with spirituality in its widest sense of where we are coming from. This is spirituality with a small *s*. There is another aspect of spirituality that deals with where we are headed as persons converted to Jesus and his way. And this is the ordinary or at least the usual meaning of spirituality. In this sense (Spirituality with a capital S) Spirituality deals with a way to God, that is, some sort of systematic way of attending to God's presence in our lives. When one looks at the history of Christian spirituality, one sees that Christians had chosen Jesus' way to God, but within that way have searched out even more specific ways of going to God. And since often when one is looking for a *way* one needs a guide, some have found valuable the way described by certain outstanding guides: Ignatius, Francis de Sales, Teresa, John Wesley, Erasmus, Jonathan Edwards, Catherine of Siena, Nicholas of Cusa, and so on.

My second introductory assumption about spirituality is that the matter can be properly attended to only within the entire context of any person's life. Spirituality cannot be handed on like a lesson in a book, or even like a book itself, which we hand to someone and say, "Here, read this." Spirituality is not a matter of cut-and-dried answers, like mastering a set of concepts. My reason for alluding to such an obvious matter is that there remain many Christian adults who still want to deal with young people piecemeal, say, in nicely packaged forty-five-minute segments. They want the easy way. However, there is no easy way to foster the spiritual development of anyone. One person does not intervene in the spiritual life of another person by means of forty-five-minute classes. Rather, one does so more by a process of interaction, a total human process. The first step to wisdom in this matter is recognizing its complexity. It cannot be organized like some well-worked-out class schedule. What young people need as far as another's intervention in their spiritual development is concerned is adults who will keep faith with them. "KEEPING FAITH WITH YOUNG PEOPLE." I want to use that expression in two senses: of adults keeping their faith in the possibilities of young people and of adults keeping their own faith as a faith to be shared with young people.

Think about your own spiritual development. Who were the persons who were decisive in your spirituality? Who have been your trusted guides? Who for you have been the guru figures? Think over that question and see if those persons were not the very ones I have described: those who kept faith with us in two senses. The danger that I try to point out to catechists and anyone else intervening in the faith life of others is that there is a way of dealing with matters of

Christian faith that blocks the experience of the ineffableness of God, that blocks them from experiencing that God is beyond words.

My third introductory point for correct thinking about spirituality is that one cannot be concerned about the spirituality of teens without being at the same time concerned about the spirituality of the entire community. One of the chief insights of the current phase of the catechetical renewal is that the chief catechizing agent is not the teacher or catechist but the community of the faith-filled. The message embodied in a community's *WAY* is more powerful than any message in a textbook or on a blackboard. And is not this the problem that persons dealing with youth have been encountering again and again in recent years: finding a community that will embody the gospel in such a way that young people can recognize the presence of Jesus?

We need communities that will keep faith with youth in both senses: keeping their faith in the possibilities of youth and also sharing their own lived faith with teens. Both senses are important, but the need for a community to keep faith with the possibilities of young people is *very* important. Otherwise many youth feel they are not needed or are only tolerated or are under constant suspicion. In one of his essays, Karl Rahner stresses the importance of Christians taking the proper stance toward the possibilities of other persons. He calls for

> The attitude of love towards, and faith in the hidden truth and the unity inherent in that truth which is in one's fellowman and which underlies all his contradictory opinions, opinions which we cannot ourselves accept. This, therefore, is truthfulness considered as openness and sensitivity to the truth which is in another, which has not yet emerged into his explicit awareness but is still concealed under what may in certain circumstances seem to be in contradiction of it.[19]

When communities have this attitude of openness toward young people, then there is the possibility of those communities becoming points of orientation for youth in continuing to search out the way to God. Such a community's own spirituality is one characterized by an on-going search for fidelity to the gospel.

These then are some assumptions about spirituality, both with a small *s* and with a capital *S*, that I see as important for fostering the proper attitude toward the spirituality of teens. They form the background for the following suggestions for dealing with the spirituality of teens.

Suggestions for Assisting the Spiritual Development of Teens

The first suggestion is: Attend to their history. A person's history more than anything else tells us where a person is coming from. It gives the trajectory of a person's life, that is, not just where the person is coming from but also the angle of the person's move into the future.

Human beings are constantly in transition. We are becoming more and more aware of this fact. But teens are in a period of intense transition, a time of passage from one stage of life to another. They are journeyers, and their spirituality will have the characteristics of the journeyer. Now in the Judeo-Christian tradition there is a time-honored spirituality of journeying: from Abraham called to move to a new country to the entire people called to be on the move through desert regions to God knows where. It is a spirituality of trusting that God does know where. I find that many adults find these images of journeying intensely meaningful in describing their own spirituality. My hunch is that a journey-spirituality is an appropriate one for young people.

It is not especially easy to attend to the histories of young people. To do so involves paying lots of attention, close attention. It takes much careful listening and what I would call "embodied interest," a kind of interest in young people that is perceived by them as a loving/freeing interest and not a controlling nosiness. It means attending to the following questions (without necessarily asking them quite as explicitly as I am going to state them).

- What has it been like for you, this journey you have been on?
- Where do you think you are headed?
- Who have been the most important who's in your life so far?
- What aches and pains have you had?
- What has helped you be most alive on the journey? What have been the spectacular sights that took your breath away?

- What in your journey so far do you most prize? Of what are you most proud? What would you never want to have done differently?
- What are your dreams for the future?
- What matters preoccupy your imagination?
- What do you want your legacy to the race or to your loved ones to be when you are gone? What do you want to stand for?
- What has the religious dimension of your life been so far? What has the Christian dimension been?

Not all these questions can be asked explicitly, but the matters behind them get at the history of young people and also at the kind of lived spirituality they now have. We can reach some understanding of the matters behind these questions by looking for clues.

- What are the clues in their humor?
- What are the clues in their worries?
- What clues might there be in the movies they see, the songs they like?
- Which works of art move them most?

To understand such matters in another human being demands a quality of openness and attentiveness that not all persons are capable of. The attitude of mind I am suggesting here is what I call the attitude of the profound stranger.

My second suggestion is to help young people move toward a spirituality that will allow for a redirected life of fantasy and playfulness.

Nobody lives without fantasy. The marketeers are handing on fantasies all the time but they are all "having" fantasies, that is, fantasies of possessiveness; and an alienating possessiveness: "I will have mine, my possessions, against others having theirs." The marketeers seem bent on handing onto us a set of values that can only alienate us from other sisters and brothers. They are bent on orienting us toward grim achievement and away from playfulness. I want young people to understand that most of the things the marketeers are trying to sell us are already ours for free if we are only willing to see them and to seize them: play, freedom, joy in friends, the ability to touch each other deeply.

A redirected life of fantasy will allow young people to long for a different set of needs—to opt for the kind of playfulness found only in persons who have a light grasp on things and consequently an openhanded approach to other people. My judgment is that Christian faith leads to this stance of the light grasp. Hugo Rahner puts it this way: "Existence is a joyful thing, *because it is secure in God;* . . . it is also a tragic thing because freedom must always involve peril."[20] Is it not true that there is a kind of trustingness in God that leads us to be authentically free and released from staking our existence on things?

I want, in summary, to encourage young people to develop the human qualities described in the following passage from Susanne Langer's *Philosophy in a New Key:*

> I believe there is a primary need in man, which other creatures probably do not have, and which actuates all his apparently unzoological aims, his wistful fancies, his consciousness of value, his utterly impractical enthusiasms, and his awareness of a "Beyond" filled with holiness.[21]

My third suggestion for those assisting the spiritual development of teens, assisting them toward a spirituality that is Christian and suited to the present day and their own present level of development, is to pay attention to a spirituality of patience. Young people need to be tolerant of their own gradualness, of their own step-by-stepness. I am talking here about a spirituality of gradualness. God's work in the lives of any of us is lifelong and cannot be prodded the way we prod a herd of cows to move quickly across a country path. (Of course, the importance of a spirituality of gradualness holds true for adults also. In fact, if we haven't learned it ourselves we will never be able to teach it to young people.)

The matter of patience with, or even better an appreciation of, and an *embracing* of our gradualness, is a profound issue that most of us must learn over and over again in our own lives. It is tied to the sense we have that God is indeed involved in our history and leading us to himself. Henri Nouwen, in one of his essays, writes about how important this matter is:

> There is a way of living in which nature becomes transparent and starts teaching us about our life and our death, about the

flow of our existence. It teaches about suffering and it teaches about joy for those who pray and for those who are constantly willing to see that life is a gift of God and experience that in the center of living.

Not only nature, but also history. Our history can be very, very opaque. For many people their life is not much more than a randomly organized series of incidents and actions, incidents and actions randomly organized of which they are sort of a part. That means for many people life is no more than chronology.

Chronos, time is *chronos.* We are just living a chronology. That makes the events of our life remain opaque. We cannot understand what really is happening. Quite often we even feel that our life is not much more than a series of interruptions.

But somewhere we have in our minds somewhat of an ideal of what real life is supposed to be. We have that ideal somewhere. "Well, we should be healthy, have a good career, go on . . ." We have plans about health and happiness and joy that we feel we should have.

But as soon as we start living, we get interrupted constantly. Something happens. Somebody gets sick in the family. "Well, that wasn't part of my plan." Or, there's a war going on or inflation or recession or something. We say, "Well, it shouldn't be there. Let's get it out of the way and get back on the track. Back, back to my ideal."

We keep not looking at those things that happen, those disturbing interruptions and keep going. And as long as we do that our life is opaque. It's dark. We don't understand.

The great conversion of our life which makes all the difference to you and to me is when life is no longer *chronos* but becomes *kairos*—that's a Greek word for opportunity—the opportunity to change your heart and your mind. That's the great conversion, when I no longer see the interruptions as disturbances but as the great chance, as the moment in which God is molding me and giving shape to my life. I have to start listening very carefully. "Why did that illness come in my life? Why is war going on? Why are all those things happening to me?"

They should not be avoided as disturbing interruptions but they slowly should be understood as a continuing challenge to change my heart and my mind, as the molding hands of God who is trying to tell me something. Can I listen, can I hear?[22]

We who would be trustworthy guides for young people must have learned some of the life vision Nouwen recommends. Only then can we encourage young people to the sort of patience needed at their

stage of development. Many are the implications of understanding
and being open to the gradualness of any person's progress. One area
where this patience must be exercised is with regard to the sexuality
of teens.

In almost every area of life, most of us have a sense that one learns
by doing. We learn by mistakes. This is what apprenticeship is all
about—guiding someone to master a skill by overcoming errors one
step at a time. Every parent knows that a child learns to walk amid
a thousand falls and the thousand bruises that go with them.
However, we tend not to apply this insight to teen sexuality. We
seem to think that a person must somehow achieve mastery and
perfection in this area with no errors. There is to be sudden and full
mastery, devoid of any incompleteness.

Obviously the area of one's exercise of sexuality and genitality is
beset with grave risks and characterized by much complexity.
Without wishing to deny these facts, I do wish to call attention to
extending a spirituality of patience to the area of sexuality. The
young people I meet, especially at the college level, need to be
encouraged to forgive themselves for some of their sexual errors.
Such self-forgiveness, and recognition that the human condition
embraces this area of their lives, might be the very posture that will
allow a young person to risk other efforts to love in a trustworthy and
responsible way.

In *Struggle and Fulfillment* Donald Evans describes how
patience "works" in interpersonal encounters and thus gives us a
glimpse of how a spirituality of patience in adults can be modeled
for teens:

> Patience is not a matter of standing to one side, passively waiting
> for the other person to start moving. It means being actively
> present to her while granting her her own time in which to grow,
> her own space in which to think and feel, her own room in which
> to find herself, her own rhythms in which to change. Indeed, I
> do not "grant" her these things, for they are already her own.
> Insofar as I am genuinely patient, I help her to *find* them and to
> *claim* them. Patience is not only a matter of reticence, not
> rushing in where angels fear to tread. It also means actively
> helping the friend to discover and create her own path in life. . . .
> It is not only a matter of conceding to a friend the right to be a
> separate person. It also means being a presence which
> encourages her to develop in her own distinctive way.[23]

Readers will recognize how much easier it is to set up prepackaged programs for teens, including Christian education programs, than it is to attend to their spirituality, which is a matter transcending any particular program, a matter of the direction of their whole lives. If spirituality is about the way we walk, where we walk, with or among whom we walk, and what we are walking toward, then adults must attend to their own spirituality in the process of aiding the spiritual development of teens. Young people need trustworthy guides, men and women of wisdom, who understand the limits of particular programs and yet who will use programs to establish a significant relationship with teens. We are all called to greatness by the Lord and any direction in spirituality by which we call one another to this same greatness is the right direction.

7

Speaking to the Songs

Persons interested in the healthy development of young people, and with establishing for them sensible protections from unhealthy influences, are becoming more and more concerned about the sexual manipulation of youth in our society. In September 1979, Women against Pornography assembled in New York City a distinguished group of feminists for a two-day conference to discuss pornography as a feminist issue of national proportions. Billed as the East Coast Feminist Conference, the gathering attracted over seven hundred women to reflect on the dominant antiwoman dimension of pornography. They heard Gloria Steinem explain that originally pornography described women as captives or slaves. "Pornography is the instruction; rape is the practice, battered women are the practice, battered children are the practice," she charged.

The conference set out to expose the public demeaning of women and of the relationship between the sexes. Conference speakers pointed out the big profits in the $4 billion a year distribution system of these cheaply produced materials. They also stressed the need for women to become politically active in opposing sexual oppression through pornography. Civil libertarians Susan Brownmiller, Bella Abzug, Gloria Steinem, and Lois Gould did not hesitate to publicly call into question the portrayal of women as those to be used and abused. Civil freedoms advocate Bella Abzug contended that freedom of the press did not prevent persons aware of the harm of pornography from raising consciousness about these dangers.

Particularly significant in the 1979 conference, and also in the preconference walking tours of the porno palaces in the Times

Square area, was the rationale used to object to pornography. Again and again the women pointed out they were solidly in favor of sex but just as solidly opposed to sick brutality that has nothing to do with sex. This rationale of opposing the dehumanization of women but not opposing sex must now be extended to a particularly difficult problem affecting youth: the kind of music young people are exposed to. Possibly feminists against pornography can give us some useful clues on how to raise consciousness about some of the callous and even brutal attitudes being expressed in some current disco music. What music? Music that delivers messages like these:

- a man telling a woman to make sure she's out of his sight the morning after they have made love ("Stay with Me" by Rod Stewart)
- a man telling a woman that all he wants from her is sex—no other attentions are welcome ("Beast of Burden" by The Rolling Stones)
- a man complaining about the money, clothes, and children that women have given him without his consent, and using racist stereotypes to describe sexual demands he does not care to meet ("Some Girls," by The Rolling Stones)
- a song implying that the only place for a woman is "between the sheets" ("Nasty Habits" by The Rolling Stones)

There are serious difficulties in responding properly to these songs. Specifically, how does one who cares about young people, who does not want to be perceived as antisex, who has deep religious convictions, and who vigorously supports civil liberties—how does such a person deal with the issues hidden behind songs like these? My own judgment is that one accomplishes nothing by expressing one's objection through the religious indignation used by an official of the New York Archdiocese, who labeled Billy Joel's cynical *Only the Good Die Young* as "an obscene, immoral, and blasphemous song."

Shrill religious wrist-slapping is an inappropriate response from spokespersons for religious points of view. Enough people in our society already perceive religious persons as asexual or at least as not fully open to the sexual. (See Isaac Singer's novel, *Shasha.*) If it is true that religious figures have tended to adopt an unhelpful moralizing stance toward matters sexual, it is also true that such a stance does not fully reflect religion's appreciation of sex. In our society, for example, Christians and Jews would do well to select the aspects of modern music that are objectionable from a humanist standpoint and begin to collaborate with other persons who are alert to these same problems. On several related issues I find myself much more willing to work with certain well-informed feminists—no matter what their religious convictions—than with some religious representatives. What are these issues which could focus the efforts of a broad coalition of persons concerned for youth?

The first issue is the continued manipulation of the unsophisticated, a manipulation that deals with teens at their most vulnerable point, that is, their emerging curiosity about sexual matters, their irrepressible sexual energy, and their eagerness to deal overquickly with several life-defining tasks, one of which has to do with sexual identity. In this matter, more than in any other of their lives, young people are open to manipulative exploitation.

Some persons will say, as several have said to me recently, that youth have always exhibited intense sexual curiosity and have always relished the media that met their needs. One can admit the truth of this statement and still insist that the quality of the titillation that youth are exposed to, and the perniciousness of its underlying message, has taken a quantum leap in the past seven or eight years. Not to be overlooked in this quantum leap is the very early age at which the sexual curiosity of some is being piqued.

If I were a woman of eighteen and heard Donna Sommer emitting the moans of orgasm in *Love to Love You Baby*, I might laugh off whatever titillation is there and go about my business. However, if I were an eighteen-year-old woman and realized that my younger sister (or my sisters in the wider human family sense) of ten or eleven was listening to the same orgasmic sounds at 33⅓ rpm on after-school radio, I would be concerned indeed. At least I would wonder what effect such bedroomalia might have on a very young woman at the edge of puberty. And if I were eighteen and realized that many other songs are like *Love to Love You Baby*, in that they are written by males but put in the mouth of a woman, my concern would be even greater. If I were eighteen and a woman, male fantasies being mouthed by women might just set my teeth on edge.

The issue here is obviously not to deny teens their legitimate sexual energy or its true earthy power. The issue is rather one of blowing the whistle on those who are setting out before children offensive and distorted ideas about sexuality and about the meaning of the relationship between the sexes. We have already worked out some protections for children with regard to films and television. However, on recordings a barnyard approach to sex is tolerated and some of the worst mutual misuses of men by women and women by men are celebrated.

Another issue is that of consumer protection. The consumer protection movement in the United States has already worked out ways of safeguarding children from dangerous products hawked by callous adults. Each year at Christmastime warnings go out to parents to beware of poorly made, potentially dangerous toys capable of maiming a child. Thanks to consumer activists, many people are leery of fast-sell artists pedaling lethal junk as playthings. The young need protection from harmful playthings, be they toys or music. The antiwoman attitudes in Meatloaf's *Paradise at the Dashboard*, thinly disguised under a layer of humor, present a lethal distortion of human reality that catches young people unaware.

This analogy between dangerous toys and woman-degrading song lyrics is not so farfetched, as can be seen in Andrew Kopkind's analysis of disco for the *Village Voice* in 1979. Entitled "The Dialectic of Disco," his article described the slick marketing techniques of the entrepreneurs at Casablanca Records, who produce not only songs but instant stars to sing them. Kopkind wrote, "Disco, first of all, is not a natural phenomenon in any sense. It is part of a sophisticated, commercial, manipulated culture that is rooted exclusively in an urban environment. Disco music is produced in big cities and its fashions are formed in big cities, at considerable expense, by high-priced professionals."[24]

To point out any of the above relationships to consumer protection is not however to advocate censorship. I doubt that censorship is the answer. Instead, some persons must match the cynical exploitation of youth with cynical attention to the bad faith and the bad taste and the fast buck tactics of those who cash in on kids. In early 1980, on prime-time TV, Donna Sommer appeared in her own hour-long special which for its first act featured her singing in a church choir in Boston where she grew up. Anyone familiar with this "artist's" songs can point up the cynicism of this portrayal. Good little girl, lovely little girl, holy little girl, standing with the choir, hands clasped at her breast, singing the praises of the Lord, sweet pigtails and all. Such goodness, such talent!

Though censorship is not the answer, the use of public airwaves in ways that do the public a disservice is a question that ought to be raised. If the TV industry could provide protection for children during prime-time evening hours, then perhaps the after-school airwaves could regulate the airings of songs with distorted sexual messages. I would expect some disc jockeys, concerned for youth, to support such a move. At least I would hope that groups of concerned persons might put pressure on the stations and their advertisers to halt the assault of aural porn aimed at early teens and preteens.

In some ways the most important issue is one of developing a consciousness about such issues among the young. That matter should be an important one for those in any way responsible for educating or raising consciousness among young people. For many youth, the subtle sexual oppression they experience through some music is beyond their awareness. The work of opening them to name this oppression will not be accomplished easily, especially not by older persons perceived as hostile to "their" music. However, even a necessary beginning will not be made unless youth workers pay more attention to the things youth pay attention to. I have been astonished in conversations with teachers and others who intervene in the lives of young people at how totally many of them overlook movies, magazines, and music, each of which has impact on the attitudes of the young. Overlooking these influences involves also overlooking an important underlying question: Who profits from the manipulation of young people?

Consciousness-raising is tied to politicization. The nonpoliticization of youth may ultimately be the most pressing issue affecting the teens of our time. Teens tend to be completely naive about the structures that affect them and about the power they themselves award to these structures and the persons working through them. The twelve-year-old who purchases a record which demeans her personhood has been doubly oppressed. She helps maintain a Mick Jagger or a Keith Richard in the style to which he has become accustomed, and she contributes to the perpetuation of a cultural attitude which demeans her. Of course a politicized youth will want a say in shaping all the structures that affect them, including the schools, which may be one reason why teachers seem to have little time to help young people understand the workings of power.

On the music issue at least, the politicization of youth might most readily take root among teen women, since they are the ones who have the most to lose. They are the ones being most demeaned by the music; they are the ones to face the agonizing questions about life and death in a socially awkward pregnancy; they will suffer the most abuse from the males who have absorbed the antiwoman messages of disco. Since women have the most to lose, they also have the most to gain by taking to the streets to voice their outrage and to demand change in the structures fostering their oppression.

Someone will ask why I have not mentioned parents in these reflections. The reason is not that I see parents' concern as unimportant, and not that their help is not needed on the issues outlined here. My reason for not dealing with them specifically is that my focus here has been on enlisting the aid of persons outside the home in attending to one aspect of the sexual oppression of teens. My hope is that as parents take action along with others to correct the injustices described here they will do so, not just because of their own children, their own sons and daughters, but because of their larger commitment as adults to hand on to the next generation, to their younger sisters and brothers, a sexual legacy of sanity and goodness, one that sees the possibility of mutuality between the sexes.

8

Youth Catechesis
in the '80s

For the past five years I have been watching youth catechesis throughout the country and have become increasingly uneasy about our directions.

My uneasiness can be directly stated in the following bald way: *Youth catechesis in this country has practically died and it has happened during the past ten years.* How did it happen? The irony is that it happened in the name of youth ministry. I would like to sketch what has happened in Catholic youth work over the past decade as a groundwork for some suggestions about the directions we should take for the new decade.

In the early '70s, Catholics found fewer and fewer young people going to what was then called high school CCD classes.[25] The older the young people got, the more dramatic the drop-off in attendance. Each year after age fourteen, there was a doubling and tripling of the dropout rate. Some felt that the teens were trying to teach us something about themselves and about the nature of ministry to them. At that time, most dioceses had two programs for youth not in Catholic high schools: CCD and CYO, and in most places these two programs were going their separate ways with little collaboration.

Out of this situation of massive resistance to catechesis in once-a-week classes developed the concept of a comprehensive ministry to youth. Ministry was a concept that was "in the air" at that time. Some theorized that the proper place for youth catechesis was within a total ministry to young people. Such thinking emerged from an understanding of how the various ministries relate to each other. In an effective effort with youth, all the ministries had to be attended to: ministry of the word; ministry of worship; ministry of guidance, counsel, including education; and the ministry of healing.[26] Further, many came to believe that for youth a primal ministry underlying and making possible the four major ministries, was the ministry of friendship.[27]

Implied in this kind of thinking was a program of meeting young people on their own terms and moving with them through the ties of caring. It was a program of sharing through caring. I realize that such a phrase sounds like mere word-play; yet the relationship between those two terms, caring and sharing, is far more significant than mere word-play. Those words suggest the new direction that ministry to youth took in the '70s. It was and remains an exciting, promising development.

However this development was accompanied by a problem, namely, that it did not go far enough. As a result, catechesis for teens has almost died out in many parts of the United States. Adults working by way of friendship with young people, relating effectively with them, do not always move actively enough to lead them to a deeper understanding of the meanings that bind the community together.

Communities do not cohere only through common needs. A more basic coherence is that of common understandings and common judgments based on those understandings.[28] To be a member of a community means in large part positioning oneself within the circle of the meanings the community holds in common.

Evangelization invites persons to the community of faith; catechesis explores the common faith that binds the community together. Youth ministry in the '70s tended to stop at evangelization.[29] The recent papal exhortation on catechesis, *Catechesi Tradendae*, attends to this problem as follows: "It (catechesis) must nevertheless be sufficiently complete, not stopping short at the initial proclamation of the Christian mystery, such as we have in the kerygma."[30]

In too many parishes of this country, catechesis for young people has almost ceased. When I try to find out who is doing creative catechesis in the United States, people usually give me the names of a handful of persons writing textbooks for the captive audiences: the confirmation classes and the religion classes in Catholic high schools.

Someone will say: What about the youth retreat movement? Is not that a vital catechetical effort? Do not programs like Search, Christian Awakening, Teens Encounter Christ, the Antioch Weekend, and the like, carry out a catechetical effort? I would like to comment on those questions, since youth retreats have been precisely what has awakened me to the drastic state of youth catechesis in the United States. Youth retreats or weekends of Christian living are, in my opinion, part of the problem because they have not gone far enough. They have gotten bogged down in a good thing. Let me explain.

Most youth retreats in this country are efforts at evangelization, not at catechesis. Briefly stated, evangelization is the call or invitation to those outside the circle of faith to stand within the circle of faith.[31] Evangelization has as its first goal, conversion, that is, a crossing over into the community of Jesus faith. Most youth retreats are successful ventures in youth evangelization. What they do is create a context in which a group of lively believers invites a group of somewhat undecided persons or quasi-believers to the delights of the table of the Lord.

The weekend experience tends to be exhilarating, a high, a turn-on. Whatever words we use (and some disparage all these words as pointing only to a weekend of emotionalism) they all suggest the same sort of excitement described in the New Testament Pentecost accounts. The excitement is half the joy of finding God and half the joy of being found by God-in-Jesus.

What is the problem? I say that conversion experiences are not enough. They are only the start of the process of helping persons understand more fully what they have been called to, to appreciate the full dimensions of the journey they have embarked on.

What sort of understanding of the gospel does one need today to follow Jesus in a credible way? What sort of growth in understanding during a period of time is called for? These are catechetical questions that erupt when the marvelous songs and the joyful handholding of a weekend are over. Right after the transfiguration, that mysterious synoptic event, Jesus led his disciples right back into the ambiguity of life and new questions (Mk. 9: 2–29); we, however, tend to leave

them tentless on the mountain. Again, in *Catechesi Tradendae,* John
Paul II insists we ask ourselves the following key question:

> How are we to reveal Jesus Christ, God made man, to this
> multitude of children and young people, reveal him not just in
> the fascination of a first fleeting encounter but through an
> acquaintance, growing deeper and clearer daily, with him, his
> message, the plan of God that he has revealed, the call he
> addresses to each person, and the kingdom that he wishes to
> establish in this world with the "little flock" of those who believe
> in him? (n. 35)

In hopes of calling more attention to the catechetical dimension of
youth ministry, I wish to propose some theses about the tasks that
face youth catechesis in the coming decade. These tasks must be
faced squarely if the progress made in youth ministry during the
past ten years is to be carried on to its next phase rather than being
blocked by our own lack of imagination or pastoral laziness. My
outline of the challenges of youth ministry in the '80s falls under
three action-oriented theses, each of which has multiple implications
at the level of special local pastoral planning.[32]

Thesis I

*Youth catechesis must retain and even extend its subject
orientation.*

One of the major shifts in catechesis-religious education during the
past twenty-five years (and unfortunately a shift that has yet to be
completed at many pastoral levels) is the shift from an object-
oriented catechesis to a subject-oriented catechesis.[33] An object
orientation in catechesis focuses on the matter to be taught, on the
content, on the objects being dealt with, that is, ideas, doctrinal
formulations and other kinds of belief-related concepts. However, a
subject orientation has its chief focus on the subjectivity at the core
of catechesis, that is, on the person of the subject being catechized.
This shift has been an enormous one, with major implications for the
entire process of catechesis.

As soon as one's central focus is on the person being catechized,
then the direction of catechesis changes from what it would be if

one's major focus was on the object or content. One becomes more concerned about the mind-set of the person, about his or her experiences of the matter being treated or discussed, and especially concerned about the person's readiness. One focuses much more in a subject orientation on the mystery of the person's own existence and on the workings of God's grace in the person's life, long before the catechist ever met her or him.[34]

A good example of the differences between a subject orientation and an object orientation can be seen in marriage preparation. An exclusively object-oriented catechesis tends toward the following approach: sit them down and tell them what they have to know and what they should believe. There is a take-it-or-leave-it attitude at the extremes of this orientation.

On the other hand, a subject-oriented catechesis focuses more on the lived experience of persons. Although subject-oriented catechesis has a clear intentionality, that is, a clear idea of its goals and where it wishes to lead the subjects, it starts with constant attention to where persons are coming from. Subject-oriented catechesis of marriage recognizes that young people already have received the great lifelong course in marriage within their families and within a particular culture. The beginning of catechetical wisdom is to recognize that fact and to have the imagination to cross over into the attitudes these young people already have toward the question of marriage. Young people have a history, and an informed catechesis involves taking this history seriously.

I say that the subject orientation of youth catechesis needs to be maintained and even extended during the coming decade. In order that we ourselves may go deeper in our own subject orientation, let us ask ourselves how we think about catechesis. How do you think about it? What are your attitudes toward it? Is catechesis, for you, dominated by concern for the mind? Is it about proper understandings or exact formulations, all those things people need to be instructed in?

I meet many persons among Catholics and Protestants alike who think that instruction is the first concern of catechesis. That view of catechesis is not so much wrong as distorted. The first concern of catechesis is not the mind or accurate formulations. The first concern is the human spirit.[35]

Catechesis is concerned with the entire human project, with the way that persons are proceeding on the journey toward becoming more human. The message given by the disciples after Pentecost was a message of new light on what it meant to be human before the Father. Once we see that the quest for humanness is at the heart of catechesis, then we cannot in our efforts with the young jump over a whole range of matters that affect the way they are becoming human beings: their music; the things the ad people are holding up for their attention and adulation; the institutions to which they must submit but in which they have no say. A subject-oriented catechesis is concerned with the human spirit and approaches persons with wide-angle vision.[36]

Let me apply subject orientation to another aspect of our work with young people. Can we properly catechize youth if we have not suffered with them? By the phrase "suffering with," I mean to extend the notion of "being with," a concept which has guided much work with youth during the past ten years in the United States. The expression "suffering with" suggests a level of compassion which enables a true crossing-over into the experience of the other person. The opposite of "suffering with" is speaking across barriers without ever stepping across them. This speaking is done with pronouncements from one, usually authoritative, perspective that is incomprehensible from the other person's perspective, especially that of the person groping for meaning in life.

Such pronouncements are imaged in Fellini's film, *8 ½*, where the distressed Guido brings his sense of emptiness to the Roman cardinal in the baths. In response to Guido's anxiety, the cardinal solemnly intones the dictum, *Extra ecclesiam, nulla salus.*

Without suffering with youth, catechetical leaders will never discover the questions alive in the hearts of young people—or of any people. They will never become privy to that edge of a person's life which opens out to the conscious need for God: joys, frustrations, incompleteness. These are the edge experiences of a person's life. In the Judeo-Christian tradition, truth and newness have been found among the marginals, among those who did not fit fixed social roles. Our youth are one such group in our society and we have much to learn from them if we have the courage to cross over into their experience.[37]

For the catechist the question comes down to this: Will we let them speak to us? Will we allow ourselves to be challenged by the dilemmas of their lives? Will we allow them to call forth from us a new response, cast in fresh and original words trying to speak to a new situation? A true subject orientation responds to these radical challenges.

As a catechist I have mastered a technical language that allows me to speak of the Christian tradition in categories quite removed from the concrete real-life situation of these particular young people here and now. I have worked to master that specialized language and in some senses I have made it mine. But if I do not have the courage to put aside that specialized language in the very interests of communication, then I cannot function as a catechist. If I simply repeat the formulations of that technical language in the face of the new situation that calls for a fresh response, then I may well be guilty of laziness. I have not faced the challenge of seeing how the tradition intersects with the lived experience of these persons. Like the cardinal in *8 ½*, I have not only not crossed over; I have responded in a foreign language that is a dead language to the listener.[38]

For me as catechist, the issue even goes beyond one of being able to communicate in words they can understand. There is another issue: Am I willing myself to learn from them and to hear what God is calling for in this new situation? Will I allow myself to be changed and made new through their marginality?

I am afraid that as I speak of these matters, my own speaking makes them seem abstract and technical. In speaking now I face the same challenge I have just finished describing. Whether I am successfully meeting the challenge or not, the issue remains as one of the radical challenges facing youth catechesis as it moves through another decade.

Thesis II

We must reverse the most common and accepted formula for catechesis.

As I see it being worked out in parishes, this formula says: Catechesis is continuous and terminal. Catechesis, according to this formula begins at about age seven and runs continuously fall semester and spring semester until the child reaches the age of about twelve or the age of confirmation or whatever the age is at which a young person can decide no longer to be part of a captive audience. For most, catechesis becomes terminal at that point.[39] Some parents become concerned about the further faith development because they recognize that for the most part catechesis does not exist for those not of the captive audiences or for those older than twenty-one.

I say we must reverse this formula about catechesis because it is a false one. It has the catechetical task exactly backward. The nature of catechesis is to be, not continuous and terminal, but occasional and lifelong. All the interventions needed to foster insight into one's faith cannot be made before age seventeen. Faith questions erupt in the lives of persons and communities and must be dealt with as they arise. Further, persons go through transitions that mark occasions when catechesis is needed. One such occasion is the occasion of two persons wishing to enter into a Christian marriage; other occasions are those when sickness and death disrupt our existence. Of course we also have the time-honored tradition in the church of Lent as the special time of renewal each year.

One can see that it is the "lifelong" component of the true catechetical formula that allows us to understand the "occasional" component. Occasional makes much more sense if we see that the occasions will be ones offered throughout the course of one's lifetime, as needed. Obviously, a shift from the inadequate formula of continuous and terminal to the more appropriate one of occasional and lifelong will demand a realignment of pastoral ministries in many places. The proper formula calls for much more attention to adult catechesis.

However, occasional and lifelong catechesis also calls for changes in our approach to youth catechesis. If catechesis were occasional and lifelong, persons dealing with youth would have much more patience with the gradual progress of young people. If we understood the faith development of youth as partial and gradual then we could adjust our catechesis to that particular aspect of their lives. We would not have to try too much too early or too much too insistently. We could allow our young people to move from one challenging but enriching catechetical situation or event to another.

I would go further here and repeat that the spirituality proper to youth is a spirituality that puts special emphasis on patience with gradual growth, a spirituality that deals more explicitly with the tension so many teens feel between their present incompleteness and transitions and their yearning for completeness.

Often, when I see young people celebrating with one another their own youth, one of the things they seem to be doing is saying: See, we understand one another. We understand what about us frustrates adults so much—that we are filled with unfinished business. At such moments I think I can see young people embracing each other and saying to each other: "You are all right in your incompleteness; I understand it." And when I meet the adults whom teens love I usually find them to be persons closely in touch with the gradualness of teen development but who also see that it is moving toward ever greater adulthood and completeness. Their very presence with youth is a gentle urging toward adulthood, toward becoming the whole human persons they are meant to become.

My suggestion for systematic catechesis for those older than twelve is that it should be short, occasional or seasonal, and free, that is, optional.

Thesis III

We must continue to examine the balance between youth ministry and youth catechesis.

There are dangers of gravitating toward either extreme. The one extreme is that of overcatechizing and underministering. This is the extreme that youth ministry in the past decade has done the most to correct. In 1970, the greater danger was that of focusing too much on the doctrinal needs of youth and ignoring a wider range of their other needs. When young people had a need for counsel, they were often offered only instruction or even indoctrination. Youth ministry came to see that a properly directed catechesis is one in the context of a person's whole life. It is not proper, in the name of catechesis, to screen out the rest of a person's needs. One way that youth ministry has moved away from overcatechizing and underministering has been by treating teens much more as adults than as children.

However, youth ministry must also avoid the danger of undercatechizing, and worse yet, undercatechizing in the name of ministry of friendship. Undercatechizing means not attending to questions and the need for information as they arise. Persons need to know the meanings that bind the community together. They need to be exposed to these meanings in as compelling and as truthful a way as possible. To neglect catechesis in the name of ministry is to be false to ministry. To remain at only one level of ministry when persons are ready for another step in their understanding is also to be false to ministry. Today undercatechizing has become an important overlooked problem in ministry to youth.

During the coming decade youth ministers need to pay more attention to the multiple ways and means of youth catechesis grounded in sound theory. There needs to be more experimentation with different strategies and modes of catechizing youth (and older Christians). My own hunch about what needs to be done is that the clues are hidden in the success of the weekends of Christian living.

In these weekends I find, not the only viable model of catechesis, but certainly an excellent one. In such settings catechesis finds its correct communal context. There too, instruction is blended with multiple forms of prayerful worship. These weekends are what I like to call catechesis in a celebrative mode.[40] The building of trust on such weekends allows catechesis to be more fully realized as dialogue, so that the participants search out for themselves the connections between the word of God and the contours of their own lives.

However, as good as I find these weekends in their catechetical components, when I look at the total youth-weekend development during the past fifteen years, I am disappointed. They have, in general, gotten comfortable and have bogged down in their own successes. Most youth-retreat programs now in use in the nation are conversion weekends. Too few of these programs have second- and third-level weekends that allow for the sort of deepening of one's understanding of the Christian message that effective catechesis demands.

I think we have the capacity of designing weekends around a myriad of important issues and themes, using the same basic formats currently being used by the conversion-type weekends, that is, formats involving oral catechesis in the context of in-depth interaction between the community of the team and the community of the participants. Such interaction leads to a single community of faith. Let me suggest some possible themes for these weekends in hopes that all of us can think more along these lines in the months to come.

I will begin my overview of the kinds of weekends I think we need by sketching a series of weekends on social justice. This is a catechetical matter, because not to know the social justice dimensions of our faith is to be badly informed about the meaning of Christian faith in the current world.

During the past ten years the majority of persons I have met who work with young people functionally ignore the wider issues of global awareness and social justice. With a few exceptions, the Catholic high schools have avoided these issues, but not to the degree they have been ignored in youth ministry outside the schools. My judgment is that young people need to be helped to this kind of awareness now more than ever. I despair of helping young people move away from the myths of privatization and nonresponsibility unless we in youth ministry face up to a catechesis for social justice. According to the 1971 synodal statement, "Justice in the World," action on behalf of justice is a constitutive dimension of the Christian message. Obviously information and understanding are important for effective action.

Recently, when I have spoken about a catechesis for social justice, listeners have more than once objected that the personality structure of the teen is too fragile to be able to cope with these massive world problems. We may be dangerously increasing adolescent anxieties, as one person put it. Much could be said on both sides of this objection; however my own sense is that this is our modern world and it does not help for any of us to bury our heads in the sand.

There is no question that an informed understanding about many social justice issues does create anxiety and turmoil. I see no way around such anxiety if we are to let our hearts be involved in a quest for a sane world. Those who in early 1980 read *The New York Times* report of what the technocrats at the Pentagon are now cooking up, not for nuclear war, but for a brand-new dish concocted of germ warfare, were, or should have been, deeply troubled. In addition there can be a condescending tone to not wanting to disturb young people as if they were children too young to understand. Our catechesis is one for adulthood, not for infancy.

1. Here then, quite roughly sketched, are some possible weekends dealing with social justice:

a. A weekend on peace: option or imperative. Much information is available about peace-making and the heroes of peace-making, which should be shared with youth. Peter Mayer's book, *The Pacific Conscience*, is filled with marvelous testimonies to peace-making. In addition, numerous films and videotapes are also available. Our young people know only too well the rationales for war, and from infancy they have ingested the symbol system of aggression. Now it is time for us to understand the Christian option for peace and the task of seeking peace. Our presentations will not have to be only about the past or about abstractions. I have found that every time I have spoken to young people about the dangers of the violence present in their own persons, they listen and ponder knowingly.

b. A weekend on economic oppression should not be difficult to design with the aid of some of the fine media materials produced in recent years. Such a weekend could be tied to the hunger question, but obviously that question could be the topic of a separate weekend. The matter of which materials are available and most useful is one I cannot deal with here, except to say that the information is available fairly easily to anyone looking for it.

In any programs on social justice, young people will need, in addition to information, lines of response to these issues. And there is always some action that can be taken. My own hope would be that some of the young people might decide to pursue studies as a way of preparing to make a lifetime contribution to relieving some aspect of human misery. Also, on these weekends I would devise periods of silent group prayer during which all present could center themselves on some kind of solidarity with the oppressed.

2. In addition to the social justice weekends, I will sketch a series of weekends on other catechetical matters:

a. A weekend on the person of Jesus as the focus of the Christian community. Such a weekend could combine doctrinal instruction on the Jesus of history and the Christ of faith with some testimonies from persons about the difference Jesus makes in everyday living. There might also be focus on the various images of Jesus that represent our complex tradition about him. It might be possible to suggest a program of gospel-centered prayer for the week and months following such a weekend. Young people could be encouraged to find the image of Jesus in the New Testament that most appeals to them and then to reflect and pray over this image for a certain period of time, possibly with the aid of a journal. I would expect the eucharistic celebration on this weekend to have special power.

b. A Jesus weekend might possibly have to be preceded by one that gives young people the basic interpretive skills to enable them to read *scripture* in a nonfundamentalist way. The matter is not so complicated that a team of skilled persons cannot lead a group to understand scripture in its true beauty as a human document that evolved over time, shaped by multiple persons and communities. This weekend would also have to be celebrative, allowing teens to sort out the different influences behind a particular text to interpret their own lives. Such a weekend would be a celebration of the power, the "rousability" of God's word.

c. I can envisage a weekend dealing with the matter of *ritual,* first as an everyday human reality and then as a reality of special importance for religious persons eager to express their faith, and finally as a privileged way that Christians allow themselves to be in communion with the mystery of Jesus' presence in their midst. Of course on such a weekend one would not make the mistake of merely talking about ritual. One would do ritual and come to testify in one's own words to its power.

3. In addition to the above weekends on specific doctrinal themes—and there could be an endless variety of possible doctrinal themes—the kinds of weekends I myself would most want to work with would deal with matters that are highly theological but not directly doctrinal.

a. The first would be a weekend that would give teens a *visual education*. Of all the gifts I would wish to give today's young people, so manipulated and, yes, assaulted by images all their waking hours, one of the chief would be a critical visual and aural sense, so they could evaluate what they see and hear. Most teens, and most adults for that matter, do not know how to see what they are watching. I would wish to work out a weekend of visual liberation because I see the matter as an important one for establishing a critical consciousness in young people.

b. My concern for the next kind of weekend comes from teaching a course in Christian marriage at the undergraduate level. I have come to see that some young people in their late teens and early twenties need a weekend of reflection on the *meaning of friendship* and its Christic dimension. This weekend would examine the question of having nonexploitive friendships across sexual lines. I meet many youth who feel they have been betrayed in friendships, and often enough they themselves have in turn betrayed others.

These are important matters at such an age and light can be shed on them by persons of wisdom and learning. The engaged encounter weekend, so many months before a wedding, is too late to handle so many of the issues related to friendship. I wonder what would happen if young people began to see marriage in continuity with their other friendships, rather than, as most of them do, in radical discontinuity with ordinary friendships. Even coming to see marriage as a friendship would be an important step in the right direction.

c. We need also to experiment with weekends dealing with *sexuality* and issues related to sexuality. Probably those between eleven and fourteen need these weekends more than others, but we have not done enough to know for certain. I would always begin by informing parents on the goals and content of the weekend and by providing some avenue for parental involvement. For the youngest to participate, parental involvement would be a requirement. Nancy Hennessey Cooney of the Milwaukee Youth Office is the pioneer among Catholics on this matter, and she is trying to network with others interested in giving a catechesis for sexuality more attention.[41]

These then are some suggestions for youth catechesis as it moves into a new decade. We cannot afford to rest on our laurels and take too much comfort in our past successes. Laurels tend to dry up and fade, and right now much remains to be done. I realize I have come to you filled with ironies; on the one hand affirming progress in youth ministry, on the other complaining that catechesis has been neglected; on the one hand calling for more catechesis, on the other asking that it be gradual; on the one hand, asking for better catechesis, on the other asking that it be occasional rather than continuous; on the one hand, focusing on youth catechesis, on the other hinting throughout that the rightful place of youth catechesis is within an intergenerational catechesis for the entire community; on the one hand having many things to say about young people as individuals, on the other having a sense of urgency that we avoid an overly individualized catechesis that ignores social justice issues.

These ironies and the multiple truths hidden in them should give us a good deal to ponder as we plan youth catechesis for a new decade.

9

Youth Ministry:
Toward Politicization

A significant danger in any ministry to youth has been and continues to be the domestication of young people and the trivialization of the teen years.[42] In order to lay these issues before you in an orderly manner, let me begin with two theses.

1. Young people in our society are among the most oppressed and manipulated segments of the population. They are oppressed because they are voiceless and therefore powerless; they are manipulated because they are unaware of the structures and systems that control their lives. These structures and systems include the educational structures, the economic structures, especially the structures for marketing and advertising; the entertainment industry, especially its subset, the music industry; the religious structures, particularly parish and diocesan organizational structures; and the political structures, especially as they affect the potential militarization of our young men and young women.

2. Youth ministry has not yet moved on to the next stage in its evolution. Youth ministry has spent the last ten years working out a revolution in the way church groups approach young people. What had been an ill-coordinated focus on exclusively instructional matters on the one hand and exclusively recreational activities on the other became a well-orchestrated ministry to a more total range of youth's needs: what we have come to call "total youth ministry."[43] We agreed with Merton Strommen that the fundamental ministry with youth is the ministry of friendship,[44] and we moved then to build our work with youth basically as a work of healing. We went

further. We stated unabashedly that the foundation of youth ministry is relational ministry, not the ministry of teaching. Where the ministry of teaching is primary, young people tend to resist it. Where the ministry of friendship is primary, the ministry of teaching can make progress. Our goal has been to go with young people as their guides through difficult years, serving as sources of hope to try to augment their human wholeness and happiness. Our wish for youth and our goal in youth work has been joy and peace—if possible joy and peace in the Lord, but at any rate joy and peace.

I do not wish to turn around or deny any of these principles, which I myself have sought to explain. What I do wish, however, is to extend them and to move them to a new stage in their development. In order to do so, let me set before you in a scenario a concrete image of a specific young person I judge to be, if not quite typical, then at least not unusual. By reflecting on the situation of this young woman, we may be able to analyze a new range of issues to which youth ministry must attend.

Her name is Donna. She is fifteen. She is standing in front of the Neiman-Marcus store in downtown Dallas at 11:30 A.M. on a Wednesday morning in October, looking into a window. It is warm, and she is in white cutoffs, a purple tube top, and sockless jogging shoes. Her hair is caught close to her head with an elastic and falls in a pony tail. She is of average height, average weight, average attractiveness, and under her average right arm she carries a neat flat package from a nearby record store. It is a school day and Donna is truant—with a vengeance.

She had attended school the day before with her homework done for the first time in several days—but when it came time to present it in English class it was gone. She thinks someone may have stolen it. Whatever happened to the homework, what happened to Donna was that she ended up in what she calls the Lady Sheriff's office, which is actually the office of the Dean of Students, the same place she had been the previous Friday for not having done her homework. This time, however, she had done it and so insisted until she got into an argument with the dean, an argument she lost when suddenly she was suspended and sent home.

Donna didn't tell her mom or dad, whom she loves, because she was afraid it would mean big trouble; and so she just skipped. Why should she go back to school anyway, she thought to herself, when all they do is call you a liar and then make up lies about you? Besides it wasn't fair to have happened yesterday, when she was already upset for another reason: she was worried she might be pregnant. So today she stands before Neiman-Marcus clutching her new Rolling Stones album and looking into the window with tears in her eyes. No, the tears are not about her injustices of yesterday or about her coming troubles. She sees a beautiful dress, just like the one she had seen in *Seventeen*. The girl wearing it in *Seventeen* was her height and her coloring and looked beautiful. But the dress in the window is marked $175.00, so far beyond anything she can afford that it hurts to tears.

What do you make of Donna and her situation? What does she say to you as a youth minister, as a person committed to the growth of young people? If you had to do an analysis of her situation for yourself, or in conjunction with some fellow adults committed to youth, and then develop some strategies for addressing her situation, what would your strategies be?

I wonder if your experience has been like that of other full-time persons in youth ministry when I asked them to discuss Donna's situation? Almost all of them said they could not discuss her situation fully because they did not have enough information. They insisted on more information. Here are some of the questions they asked.

—Who are her friends? Are they a good or a bad influence? Can they be brought in as an aid to her or are they such a bad influence that she must break away from them if there is to be real change?

—What is her IQ? Does she have a good relationship in general with her teachers? How does she feel about school? Is she in any extracurricular activities? Does she want to go on beyond high school or does she want to drop out?

—What does she do for counseling? Can she talk to her parents? Is she in touch with any adult who can function as an advisor? What about her church or synagogue? Does she have one and if she does, does she attend?

—Why does she think she is pregnant? It it because she has physical clues such as having missed her period, or is she sexually naive? How sexually active is she?

—Does she have any brothers and sisters? How much spending money does she get? How does she get along with her parents? What kind of person is the guy with whom she's involved.

These are the kinds of questions my scenario triggered. As one person put it, "You gave us a scenario and asked us to evaluate the young woman's situation, but actually you told us almost nothing about her." They agreed that until they knew more particulars they understood very little.

However, I had deliberately arranged the scenario so as to give a range of significant information about Donna, never intending to reveal her intimate, personal, psychological situation. I wanted to get at her social situation and at some of the social structures she deals with or, better put, that deal with her. All the youth ministers I have shared this scenario with tended to think exclusively in psychological terms. They overlooked any other dimensions of the matter. Let us go back and examine the kind of information given in the scenario.

—Donna goes to school. She is in her tenth year of compulsory schooling. She has been at it ten long years, and the compulsion she is under to attend is no "paper compulsion"; her truancy is a legal offense that can spark state interference in her life. She can be locked up for it.[45] She spends five hours a day in an institution where she, like her fellow students, is powerless and tends to succeed best when she questions structures least. Within that system she has just been treated unjustly. She was falsely accused and when she tried to defend herself, she was summarily suspended. There was no hearing; the hearing will come when one parent—and possibly both—takes a day off from work to accompany her to the school to discuss her suspension and possibly her further punishment. (Of course, the dean possibly could admit to Donna and her parents that she, the dean, had been having a difficult day and had reacted unreasonably and hastily without hearing Donna out, and for that reason wishes to apologize. I would rather not suggest this possibility lest you accuse me of being cynical).

—Donna is sexually confused, at the very least in the sense that she does not know whether she is pregnant. True, we do not know why she has this question; it could be that she is another of the young women of her age who are incredibly ignorant about their own bodies.[46] What we do know, however, is that she has been sexually titillated since she was old enough to understand what she saw on TV or question what she heard on the radio.[47] The sexual message she did not get from daytime "soaps" she would have gotten from nighttime melodrama. Perhaps she has heard another Donna—Donna Sommer—in orgasm at 33⅓ rpm or seen all the lovely possibilities of young and innocent love in *The Blue Lagoon*. Certainly she has been subject to a public barrage of erotic messages coupled with what might be considered a conspiracy of silence about sexuality from parents, school, and church persons.

—Donna is in an economic bind. She has little money but is still subject to a massive campaign by the marketing industry to manipulate her wants. A cruel hoax is being played on her. The clothes she needs to wear, such as jeans, are made into status symbols at the same time their price is tripled. In such a society, to be fifteen and to be cash poor is to be doubly oppressed. It means being highly vulnerable to manipulation around status and to be financially denied access to the symbols of status. Little does she realize the great care that went into *Seventeen* to produce exactly the reaction she had when she saw that dress in the window.

Donna, however, could afford one purchase this Wednesday morning. She could afford Mick Jagger and the Rolling Stones. She has just contributed to the support of someone whose songs are, as often as not, blatantly antiwoman. When a man sings a song he himself wrote about a woman, and the song demeans all women, then all women better take note! In his song "Some Girls" Mick Jagger sees women as manipulative destroyers who take him for all he has and leave him with venereal disease; he uses racist stereotypes to describe sexual demands he does not care to meet. In his "Live With Me" the woman's role is limited to her functions "between the sheets" and to taking care of the children and the house. In "Under My Thumb" (co-authored with Keith Richard) a gloating male revels in his dominance over a woman who depends on him for her style of life, and who therefore "does just what she's told."

Live With Me

I've got nasty habits.
I take tea at three.
Yes, and the meat I eat for dinner, it must be
        hung up for a week.
My best friend he shoots water rats
        and feeds them to his geese
Don' cha think there's a place for you
In between the sheets?
Come now, honey, we can build a place for three.
Come now, honey, don' cha wanna live with me?

There's a score of harebrained children;
They are locked in the nursery.
They got earphone heads;
They got dirty necks.
They're so twentieth century.
Well, they queue up for the bathroom
'round about seven thirty-five.
Don' cha think we need a woman's touch to make it
        come alive?
You'd look good pram pushin' down the High Street.
Come now, honey, don' cha wanna live with me?

Under my Thumb (Jagger and Richard)

Under my thumb's the girl who once had me down.
Under my thumb's the girl who once pushed me around.
It's down to me; the diff'rence in the clothes she wears
It's down to me; the change has come
She's under my thumb.

Under my thumb's a squirming dog who's just had her day
Under my thumb's a girl who has just changed her ways
It's down to me, the way she does just what she's told
It's down to me, the change has come, she's under my thumb.

Possibly Donna does not listen to the words of these songs; possibly
she is unaware of the great put-down women are receiving at the
hands of some modern music makers, including Jim Steinman of
Meatloaf, and Georgio Maroder and Pete Bellotti who write some of
the things that Donna Sommer sings. Or, possibly she does not
care.

But I care. As someone concerned with youth in our society, concerned that they have a chance to grow up without being demeaned, I care—or more accurately, I am troubled—about the music that influences, or manipulates, the consciousness of teens; I am troubled about the way teens are targeted by the advertising industry as undiscriminating consumers;[48] I am troubled about the sexual messages teens receive and the lack of dialogue about these messages. And I am also troubled at the powerlessness of teens in so many of the institutional structures that affect them, including the school and the church.

What I have been describing is a bit of the social structural situation of fifteen-year-old Donna. We do know her social situation, but we tend to ignore it or to overlook it. Possibly we consider it not very significant. I say it is keenly significant. Until we focus on the social situation of young people like Donna and allow it to become more obvious to us and confront us, our efforts to intervene in her life will be little more than band-aiding.[49]

Some readers may react to my analysis of Donna's situation by contending that there is nothing new in what I've been saying; that they have known for years about these aspects of the lives of teens—it is just the real world they live in and we have been trying to help them to live/survive in that world and even go further to human wholeness. But such a contention misunderstands what I am suggesting. I think that until active awareness of the lives of teens at the social-structural level shapes our ministry with youth, the next step in the evolution of youth ministry cannot happen. Awareness of the institutional structures that shape and sometimes oppress young people must create a new range of options in the way we actually minister to and with young people. This awareness calls for an evolutionary shift in our approach. What is the shift I am talking about? Let me describe it.

Donna's problem is not that she is manipulated by some social institutions, oppressed by others, and powerless in almost all. Her problem is that she is unaware of what these institutions are doing to her. She fully exemplifies "second naivete." First naivete is naivete about matters such as sexuality, and the phrase suggests a basic lack of information and/or understanding so often found in our youngest teens. In general, youth work is aware of first naivete, even where it chooses to ignore it. Second naivete, however, is naivete about social reality, ignorance of those not-immediately-evident structures that affect life so fully.[50] Youth work tends to ignore second naivete completely, because youth work itself is characterized by second naivete—almost as much as is Donna herself.[51]

One of the most effective ways of maintaining oppression is to disguise the oppression so thoroughly that the oppressed are unaware of it. This way is most effective because no action against oppression can be taken until one recognizes there is oppression. My youth ministry shift is one that takes seriously the task of raising consciousness among young people about the world they live in, the world that affects them. The task is not an easy one.

For almost three years I have been working to develop the consciousness of young people about popular music. At the first suggestion that some of this music is manipulative of women and demeaning of them, as well as misrepresenting what is humanizing behavior in men, most young people react defensively. "Who listens to the words anyway? What's the matter, don't you have a sense of humor? Nobody takes this stuff seriously. Hey, this is our music; you don't knock *our* music, we won't knock the Ink Spots." However, when they begin to look at the impact of some of these rhythms and ideas on very young teens and when they notice that some of the lyrics most demeaning of women are written by men who hire women to sing them, and when they see the organizational structures behind the production and marketing of this music, they begin to smell a rat. What seemed to be insignificant becomes significant. What was hidden is made more open; what was in the dark enters the light; what was unquestioned becomes suspect. An aspect of the humanly created world is put into the hands of the humans for whom it has been created, and they begin to analyze it and take it apart, and in this case, decide it is a poor product indeed.

I am suggesting here that an important but largely overlooked task of youth ministry is an educational task of raising consciousness about the world young people live in. Most young people live in a tightly circumscribed world that I call the world of the neighborhood.[52] They have emerged from the world of the *domus*—the world whose boundaries are the walls of the home—but they tend not to move beyond the neighborhood to the section, to the town or city, to the county, to the state, to the geographical region, to the nation, to the continent, to the hemisphere, to the world. What I am actually talking about is the politicization of youth.

By politicization of youth I mean more than simply the relationship of young people to different political parties. My concern is the relationship of youth to the *polis*, to the sphere of human affairs. Politicization in my sense is a work of enablement by raising consciousness about the structures that affect one's life and by encouraging lines of action to speak to these structures. The opposite of politicization is privatization and domestication, which are outcomes of ignorance and immobility. To allow young people to be ignorant of the structures and powers that affect their lives and ignorant of the orchestrated efforts to maneuver and manipulate them, is to lead them into the modern world as blind women and men, who must be led here and there, who move with steps so faltering there can be no self-initiated action on behalf of themselves and their sisters and brothers.[53]

In the past our youth ministry has not dealt with these questions. We have been operating on an assumption that the goal of our ministry is one of healing, of helping teens toward greater hope and greater happiness and a better chance of fitting in, both in the wider society and in the churches. We have laid much stress on inner peace, especially through communion with God. Such inner peace needs to be stressed for youth seeking their center during the confusing and turmoil-filled teen years. However, such a stress needs to be balanced by an equal stress, not on healing and happiness but on freedom. Once we begin attending to the freedom of teens, then we will face the task of unmasking the social structures that affect their lives so powerfully.

I am not suggesting a choice here between a youth ministry geared toward happiness and healing and one geared toward freedom. Both values are to be held firmly, both happiness/healing and freedom, but always with the understanding that as humans our vocation is for freedom, with true happiness existing as a by-product of struggle toward the authentically human. Rahner reminds us there is no authentic human act which is not grounded in freedom.[54] At least some of the unhappiness of teens comes from the structural or systemic unfreedoms in their lives.

Were her parents to call me in to give counsel to Donna, I could possibly comfort her and encourage her to go back and apologize to the dean for arguing with someone in authority and take her punishment "like a real woman." However, Donna would still remain in a triadic system where two elements of the triad, the administration and the teachers, are increasingly well-organized and sophisticated in reaching their goals and the third element, the students, tend to be powerless and voiceless in an institution claiming to have their good at heart.[55] I could also give her counsel about her developing sexuality, warning of the dangers of casual sex and advocating the value of waiting until marriage. However, I know that as long as she can go to her record player and absorb unconsciously and therefore unquestioningly the Mick Jagger philosophy on women and sex, she will remain locked in a potentially destructive situation.

Youth ministry that seduces young people to live in an ever more privatized world, unaware of and uninterested in the structures that dominate their lives, is already a heavily politicized ministry, but only in the sense that it keeps youth under tight control and legitimizes the oppression of young people by hiding it or masking it.[56] Our task is to unmask the anonymous oppressors of young people, to create a program that will allow youth themselves to cease being anonymous. Oppressors lump those being oppressed into anonymous groups and they succeed when those groups remain silent, passive, or inarticulate. The unmasking and naming of one reality, the oppressors, is useless without the unmasking and naming of the other, in this case, young people stepping forward to speak for themselves and to take action for themselves.

The fact of the matter is that youth must speak for themselves and take their own action. One can undertake liberation not in the abstract or in theory but only in concrete historical situations and in confrontation with these situations. One does this by giving up the anonymity that is both namelessness and facelessness and stepping forward to speak for oneself. In our society youth need to come forward as a group with human faces, to finally put an end to their nonthinking complicity in their own exploitation.

The old advocacy in youth ministry was one of helping youth by speaking out for them. It involved speaking for those who could not speak for themselves, either because they did not know the issues or could not articulate them or could not get a hearing. The new advocacy is one of inviting and enabling youth to speak for themselves by helping them know the issues and come to their own expression of them and get their own hearing. The new advocacy obviously involves the politicization of youth and laying the groundwork for a lifetime of critical judgment, a lifetime of having one's eyes opened. Many of the matters youth will examine in the new advocacy will not, as I am very well aware, bring them immediate comfort and rest but will bring instead challenge and restlessness.

We have invited many young people into youth ministry as our helpers and even as our peers. We have not in every case invited them into the new advocacy. Unfortunately, it is possible for a young person to assume his or her own full-time ministry with a particular church community and still never enter the world of humanly created structures or of critical consciousness.[57] If the new youth ministers duplicate the privatized consciousness of the past, then we have only compounded our problem because we have passed it on to a new generation of youth ministers. Such persons tend to operate out of a trivializing and domesticating strategy of giving comfort and entertainment to young people without giving them the tools to understand the world in which they live.

Concrete Implications and Programs

In terms of specific programs, what am I advocating? Before answering this question, let me repeat a statement of what I am not advocating. I am not advocating abandoning our significant developments in youth ministry up to now.[58] Our ministry to youth must be coordinated to meet a range of youth's needs; it must be founded on the ministry of friendship; it most properly takes place within the context of a believable community of believers; its educational programs should be undertaken in a variety of flexible modes. I am not advocating reversing any of these developments or principles.

Neither do I think anything is to be gained by banning singers like Mick Jagger or his records, or by censoring magazines read by teens. My judgment is that popular culture, even in its most manipulative aspects, is practically irreversible. My hope is that youth can be encouraged to think through for themselves a stance alerted to the manipulative and the tawdry and the fake—a stance persistently on guard against exploitation. Such a stance is certain to lead to action, though such action cannot be programmed. What we can do is show young people the possibilities of taking action in orchestrated, planned ways.

What I am advocating, then, is a more deliberate and serious approach to the task of consciousness-raising, which is seen as an educational task. Though there is an instructional component to this task, the major part of it is accomplished through a dialogue in which we engage in a mutual examination of reality. Youth ministry cannot complete this task, certainly. I am asking that youth ministry begin it by working with youth toward freedom and by laying the groundwork for a lifetime of critical consciousness.

The following two issues need to be examined by those who cherish the freedom of young people as much as their adjustment and happiness. The issues need not merely to be recognized but to be faced through systematic efforts at instruction and reading, analysis through dialogue and concrete action.

The Issue of Sentimentality

I judge that the education of the emotions should be a priority among those working with youth. Sentimentality is a reversal of our emotional response. A trivial incident evokes what seems to be deep feeling or deep concern. Sentimentality is a tendency toward emotional misjudgment or error. The danger here is that a serious matter calling for a passionate or compassionate response receives little attention and response, or even the response of a shrug. Lassie's death is a trauma; starvation, inhuman living situations, oppression, and injustice are not perceived as significant and are overlooked.

Sentimentality thrives on an idealized Pollyanna approach to life. Those concerned for the freedom of the young cannot encourage an emotional tone that is unwilling or unable to face evil and that, in order to avoid it, clings to a childish approach to reality, where every ending is happy and slick. Of course, trivial matters usually do not call for life transformation; they tend to leave our neat world intact, which may be why we prefer them.

I am not suggesting that youth ministers can turn around single-handedly the barrage of sentimentality aimed at young people especially on screen and in "soap" and song. What I do suggest is an overall distrust of sentimentality, together with an overriding concern for emotional truth. If sentiment can be evoked by carefully manipulated feeling, then at least we can move in a direction of helping youth to be on guard against it. Sentimentality has a close relationship to the second issue I wish to raise.

The Issue of an Uncritical Visual Sense

Some will be astonished at my selection of this issue as a major one for attention in any program to foster the critical consciousness of youth in our society. Ironically, in our society, dominated as it is by visual images, the very dominance of these images tends to mask their impact. At the same time that the image makers are so carefully arranging configuration, lighting, and texture of their images for their subliminal or suggestive impact, the image receivers are more and more apt to take them in without actually seeing them. To turn around the phase, "What you see is what you get," what you *don't* see is what you get. In other words you are getting impressions that you are not even aware of. Such a receiving of images without actually seeing is apparently what Jerzy Kosinski intended to satirize in his novel, *Being There*, in which dim-witted Chance, the gardener, describes his role in life as "I watch."

Young people need the freedom that can be offered them by a critical visual sense. Over ten years ago Dr. John Culkin worked to help educators develop such a visual sense, but as far as I know his programs later fell into disuse. The Television Awareness Project being promoted by the National Council of Churches is a newer effort and one that is badly needed. I have said often that if I could run a single weekend for teens, on any topic at all, the topic I would choose would not be at all directly religious; it would be a weekend devoted to fostering an awareness of images. This for me would be a first step toward an alertness to aural messages, especially those in music.

There are multiple implications to the overall issues I have raised here, but this is not the place to spell out specific programs. It is important, however, to stress that apart from any specific program,

I am advocating to youth ministry a new way of paying attention to the condition of young people in our society. Paying attention usually does not happen without a concerted effort to be alert. The task of paying attention to the situation of youth at the systemic, institutional level is for all of us a lifelong task of striving to unveil reality for ourselves.[59]

Some of what I have said here is certain to be a frustrating challenge to many because it opens up a new dimension of the problem. However, I have applied to youth ministry understandings of reality that began to be noticed and taken seriously by theology only around 1968.[60] All I want to say at this point is that if there is a dimension of youth ministry that we have tended to overlook, then let us begin to attend to it. My own hope for the decade of the '80s is that those young people who benefit by our intervention in their lives will move on to adulthood blessed with a critical awareness and an educated skepticism. What a gift for a fifteen-year-old Donna, a gift she can then hand on to others!

10

Why Johnnie and Joannie Can't/Don't Care

For the past several years I have been a teacher of undergraduate theology. Though the following examples are actual accounts from one year's experience, they are typical of the kinds of attitudes I have encountered during this period.

—After explaining an essay test to be given in a Christian marriage course, I received a strong objection from a student claiming that in the final year of his five-year pharmacy program this was the first essay test he had been expected to take. He was not pleased with this eleventh-hour opportunity to express discursively what he knew.

—In a New Testament introduction course, more than one of the first-year students could not express him or herself except in vague one-sentence paragraphs—in handwriting that itself symbolized the absurdity of the written word. They insisted that they understood the material and knew what they wanted to say but just could not express it. They assumed I would be able to understand why they could not make themselves understood. I disappointed them.

—When questioned about their reading habits, most of the students admitted that their free, uncoerced reading hovers around significant matters such as the sports page, the ads (especially those for clothes, electronic gadgetry, and cars), picture stories about so-called popular figures, and news stories dealing with violence or the bizarre.

—To these examples, I add a strong impression that the ordinary speech of most students seems never to turn to global issues, issues that affect the future of the race, but rather remains fixated at the level of local, even neighborhood, events and at the level of matters of the immediate past (what happened last weekend) and of the immediate future (what will happen next weekend or on vacation).

Perhaps this matter of the limited scope of students' concerns explains why I found myself so deeply disturbed by the film *Saturday Night Fever;* it reflects the consciousness not just of one who works in a paint store but of many who are putting in time on campuses. In *Saturday Night Fever,* Tony Manero cares or knows little of the past. He does manage to connect Shakespeare with *Romeo and Juliet* but he cannot identify Laurence Olivier. As for the future, his not-so-eloquent final word in the matter is, "Fuck the future."

The purpose of these examples is not to put down the current generation of young people but rather to alert educators and others who intervene in their lives to some neglected dimensions of their task. The students described in the above examples are young persons imprisoned in a world of immediate experience. They have not yet crossed over from their own private experience, from their own semiprivate islands, to the mainland world of human learning that represents the pooled experience of human beings and the understanding of that experience.

Bernard Lonergan describes that crossing over from the world of immediacy to the world mediated by meaning as a conversion. It is an intellectual conversion involving "a radical clarification and, consequently, the elimination of an exceedingly stubborn and misleading myth concerning reality, objectivity, and human knowledge, i.e., the myth that overlooks the difference between the world of immediacy (the world of the infant) and the world mediated by meaning." The stubborn myth here is that what is heard, seen, touched, tasted, smelt, and felt encompasses total reality. Intellectual conversion allows a person to realize that the world of immediacy is but a tiny part of the world mediated by meaning. As Lonergan explains,

> The world mediated by meaning is a world known not by the sense experience of an individual but by the external and internal experience of a cultural community, and by the

> continuously checked and rechecked judgments of the commu-
> nity. Knowing, accordingly, is not just seeing; it is experiencing,
> understanding, judging, believing. . . . The reality known is not
> just looked at; it is given in experience, organized, and
> extrapolated by understanding, posited by judgment and
> belief.[61]

The crossing over to the world of meaning is an act of freedom and
liberation. It is a liberation from a kind of solitary confinement, from
the island of an isolated existence, to the world of connectedness
found in the cultural community.

How does a person move from the solitary world to the social
world of meaning? The dominant way is through language and the
ability to use language as an expressive vehicle of communication,
especially the language we call speech. When even the handwriting
of an increasing number of students shows scant regard for the
possibilities of human communication through the written word, I
begin to grow anxious about an important aspect of the human
project. The ability to use speech effectively in communication is so
acutely lacking in *Saturday Night Fever* that it emerges as one of the
major themes of the film. In this movie the dominant language is the
language of the grunt and the cliché and the shouted obscenity and
the viscerally physical response. Nobody listens and consequently
nobody cares. Ironically, Bobby C., to whom nobody listens and who
is unable to move from the island of his alienation to a community
of care, leaps to his death off the Verrazano Narrows Bridge; he leaps
off the island-link connecting Staten Island to Brooklyn. For him the
bridge of language provided no connection but instead the precise
place of final disconnection.

Scott Hope, a colleague who teaches writing at San Francisco
State, suggests the concept of an inverted pyramid as a visual way of
describing the various types of language and the dimensions of the
world of meaning they open up for us. At the inverted apex of the
pyramid is the self. Next up the scale of language and at a wider
angle of the pyramid is family. Higher still is the language that
allows us to communicate with peers. His scale in ascending order,
and at ever wider angles of the pyramid, continues with community,
regional matters, national matters, other cultures, civilization, and
finally universal matters, including transcendence.

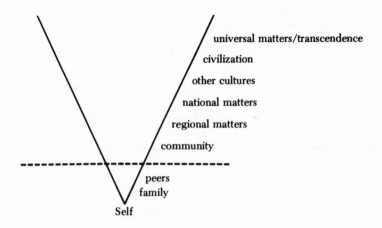

Of course, in order to deal with these various aspects of the humanly constructed world, there are several modes of communication among which one could select—verbal, visual, ritual, and so on. The arts fuse together both several aspects of the humanly constructed world and several modes of communication. Peter Schaffer's play *Equus* deals at the same time with matters of self, family, peers, language, civilization, and transcendence, all handled through that combination of the verbal, the ritual, and the visual that we call drama. The value of all the arts is their ability to connect the various human concerns and modes of communication.

What is becoming increasingly alarming for some persons dealing with students in college and high school is the limited scope of the languages they have at their command. Scott Hope puts it thus:

> Students who enter universities increasingly have available to them only those languages which allow them to communicate with themselves, with their families and with their peers. They seem to feel that they *do not need* (emphasis his) a language beyond the peer language. . . . Those of us who teach writing frequently encounter such insularity. A large, bluff student thundered at me a couple of years ago that his friends understood him so why the hell should he have to write good. Our society is dominated by peer languages, the in-languages used by educators, by sociologists, by est-graduates, by denizens of the Now society, by technicians of all stripes, by politicians, by the

Pentagon, and so on.... To repeat, then, people who do not think they need languages beyond the languages of their peers are not going to be eager to acquire the skills of those metalanguages.[62]

As does Scott Hope, I find the situation alarming but wish to stress that both his and my alarm goes beyond concern for technical skills.

The alarming aspect of this situation is not only that students do not have the skills of writing or reading, or even that they are not functioning the way "college material" should function, but that so many young people are unable to live in the wider world of human connectedness. They are isolated on an island of speech that restricts them literally (if one will allow the word's redundance in this context) to the insular world of self, family, and peers. On this island existence is alienated, cut off from important areas of the human world-mediated-by-meaning. It is also cut off from the past and shows little concern for the future.

Our alarm is actually about the concerns and the cares that occupy the attention of our young people. Language tends to be a vehicle of concern, a way of noticing and attending to aspects of life. The scope of one's meta-languages marks also the scope of one's meta-concerns. Just as one will notice only those matters within the range of one's intellectual horizon, so one tends to focus on those matters that come into the range of one's language. Language gives us a way of caring because it gives us a way of noticing and of crossing over into other concerns and more universal issues.

My concern for the writing/reading problem goes far beyond the kind of concern applauded by English teachers and beyond a reverence for the past applauded by the history specialists. My concern is for the capacity for concern. My concern is for attentiveness to the human project as it involves a world wider than those-persons-who-live-in-the-same-dwelling-as-I and who may have the same last name. My concern is about education, and it involves the entire profession of educators dealing with the young in colleges and high schools. For the teachers of writing to be preoccupied with writing skills only, without awareness of their wider implications, is for me somehow to substitute for the more important the lesser and thus to be back to the same problem. To quote Scott Hope once more: My concern as a teacher of writing is first "to expose the students to cultural universes other than those they normally inhabit, and, secondly, to expose my students to the fact that we have troubles in places other than River City."

It is one thing to develop skills in students, to "turn out" trained persons—pharmacists, accountants, or even teachers—with all the proper, carefully measured competencies. It is of a different order to lead a person to the sorts of meta-concerns that mark the educated person. Lonergan's category of conversion suggests that at the heart of education is a crossing over that each person must make for her or himself; it cannot be forced on the person through any program of training. It is relatively easy to get a degree without being educated, but one cannot get an education without being converted. Among educators themselves I find too few signs of full intellectual conversion or of these meta-concerns. So many educators seem to be so involved with their own professional peers ("my" field, "my" area, "my" subject) that they have abjured the wide-angle vision that should mark a guardian of culture, a true educator. My own hunch is that students will tend not to move beyond the languages of self, family, and peers unless educators themselves represent a community of broader concerns. For an educator to forget these broader concerns is to become more akin to an instructor in driver training or cosmetology than a guardian of culture.

At the completion of a recent semester I shared some of the above ideas with students in my marriage course. I was warning them against the *Love Story* view of marriage, against seeing it as a private venture shutting out the world. They paid close attention and found the ideas unsettling. Toward the end of the class several challenged me to tell them what I expected. Certainly, they insisted, they were preoccupied with their own selves and questions about what sort of person they wanted to be, with their struggles for intimacy especially with boy or girl friends, and with their present and future families. What were they supposed to do, go out and save the world, all with one great big sigh? At that moment it seemed to me that they were correct—to an extent.

Later I reflected on the number of these same students I had spoken with in private counseling sessions, in which again and again they seemed to have had too little perspective on their own personal problems. Even at a personal level they were in too little touch with their own past and had scant hope for the future. So many seemed to feel trapped on their own tight little island. In saying this I am not denying that the nature of personal problems tends to include a loss of perspective for any age group. I have asked myself how these students will be when they are in their forties. Will they still be reading mainly the newspaper ads, only, then, for the bigger cars and the more youthful styles—the next purchasable anodyne? I wonder if they will have any more perspective then, if now they are not challenged by education to look over fences and to move between a variety of meta-worlds. Will they end up with the blank stare and the uncomprehending chatter of Mary Hartmann?

At this point it should be clear that although I am intensely concerned with students' lack of the technical skills of writing, I do not see the writing problem as just a matter of achieving technical skills in written communication. It has much broader implications for our students and for their potential contribution to the future of the race. To neglect these broader dimensions of education is to foster among the young a kind of imprisonment in a narrow circle of concerns. We run the danger of their walking through our educational systems as the Willy Lomans of the future, preoccupied with tilling their gardens, with the narrow plots of land on which they happen to find themselves; the one difference being that these Willy Lomans of tomorrow will all have degrees.

Writing in *Harper's* a few years ago, Peter Marin put the issue this way:

> The end result of this retreat from the complexities of the world is a kind of soft fascism: the denial, in the name of higher truth, of the claims of others upon the self. . . . What is lost is the immense middle ground of human community. The web of reciprocity and relation is broken. The world diminishes. The felt presence of the other disappears, and with it a part of our own existence. The real horror of our present condition is not merely the absence of community or the isolation of the self—those, after all, have been part of the American condition for a long time. It is the loss of the ability to remember what is missing, the diminishment of our vision of what is humanly possible or desirable.[63]

Passages like this one make me sometimes suspect that, as one concerned with theology and education and *religious* education, I should not be teaching theology at all but instead teaching writing and a love for literature and the other arts. Then I realize it is not an either/or matter. I often think, too, that as one concerned about religion the greatest gift I could give my students would be an enriched imagination and that at least one night each week groups of us should perch in one or other of the Broadway theaters or at the Metropolitan Opera and allow ourselves the chance to cross over through the arts into broader human experience. At least then we could let our neat worlds be torn apart by the beauty/ugliness/irony of *Rigoletto* or the alienation theme of *Fall River Legend*. After all, we are whole persons and education should lead us back to the wholeness of experience. Ultimately such matters are a deeply religious concern.

11

Evangelization of Young Adults

Addressing the topic of the evangelization of young adults is a difficult task, especially when the meaning of the term "evangelization" is currently beset with intense "fuzzification" and when the population designated by "young adults" is broad and inexact. Before anything meaningful can be said about the topic of this article, both terms in its title must be clarified.

Evangelization

I consider some of the current literature of evangelization wrong-headed. Rather than working with the history of the term as it was developed by missionaries steeped in the catechetical tradition, some people seem to be reinventing the word so that it means anything and everything. Evangelization, as the term was used in French catechetical literature of the 1940s and 50s, was a process of leading persons to conversion to Jesus faith. These theorists understood the boundary between evangelization and catechesis to be conversion. Evangelization was the term they used for the processes that invited those outside the circle of conscious faith to move within the circle of faith, especially as that circle was embodied by a community. Catechesis was the term used for all those processes by which individuals and communities of the faith-filled grew to a deeper faith. Thus, evangelization, in its origins, had a specific delineation born of distinctions I judge to be valuable and clarifying.

This brief description of evangelization suggests that at its core it is about transformation. Basically, evangelization is a transformative category, not an affiliative one. To put evangelization into a churched/unchurched frame of reference, as does some current "evangelization bandwagon" writing, is to use an image of affiliation or, depending on perspective, one of en-listment, of putting persons back on the rolls. In a sense, the matter of en-listment is a fairly easy matter to deal with, solved by good list-makers and well-maintained addressographs.

However, once put in the context of conversion and transformation, evangelization can not be achieved in an easy manner. Conversion involves an interior change, a moving to a new perspective, analagous, according to Lonergan, to falling in love. Rallies, harangues, and traveling God-shows are not sufficient for negotiating that sort of life-change. If there were an easy way of becoming Christian, we would probably call it becoming "churched." In fact, back in the early fifth century, Augustine, in *The First Catechetical Instruction*, warned pointedly about encouraging affiliation without transformation. In an article in *Living Light*, Marjorie Moffat gives a sound reminder that some who have been converted to Christ do not want to be "churched," at least not in certain communities. Evangelization and "church-ification" are not always the same issue. What may seem at first like nitpicking distinctions become, as we shall see, important points of clarification when applied to the evangelization of young adults.[64]

Young Adults

What population are we talking about when we speak of young adults? I myself have heard the term used as the new euphemism for twelve- to fifteen-year-olds. On the other hand, Daniel Levinson's outline of the five eras of the life cycle (*The Season of a Man's Life*) puts the young adult era roughly between ages eighteen and forty-five. While most would agree that young adults are persons beyond their teens, many find they must specify the population much more narrowly than does Levinson, in order to be able to think creatively about specific strategies of ministry.

The problem of identifying specific young adult populations is not an easy one, as those who have for the past several years been serving on the USCC Working Board for Young Adult Ministry will testify. Much of their time has been spent trying to specify particular age groups and need groups that can be classified as young adults, and the task is far from finished. Those concerned about ministry to young adults will have to continue specifying the particular population they are concerned with: young marrieds under thirty; young singles under thirty; divorced persons of a particular age range; young adult homosexuals; Vietnam veterans; or the unemployed. My own use of "young adults" will refer to persons between twenty and thirty-five.

Evangelization of Young Adults

Using these clarifications as background, I approach the evangelization of young adults by way of a central thesis. My thesis turns around a common presupposition of popular evangelization writing, that is, that the persons being evangelized have everything to gain from the church, and look at the matter from what will at first appear to be a contradictory angle: *that the church has everything to gain from young adults who are being evangelized.* It should become clear that these presuppositions are complementary rather than contradictory. The following pages will examine two main assertions that support my view that young adults and the task of evangelizing them are a gift to the church: the first having to do with the liberation of ministry, the second with the conversion of the church. After explaining these two assertions in detail, I will conclude by offering four suggestions to guide the actual evangelization of young adults.

First, *evangelizing ministry to young adults will be a liberating ministry for the church.* A matter clarified by ministry to young adults is a stubborn misconception about humans and about the nature of ministry to them. It is the misunderstanding that leads us to think that persons can be marched through programs the way small children are lined up in an elementary schoolyard after recess and walked back to class. Young adults will not let themselves be marched through any program. More of this assembly line attitude afflicts persons in ministry in this country than we are willing to admit. We should not be surprised, of course, that in our country, with its penchant for technologized systems, a mechanization mentality can affect ministry, as much as it does some sectors of education (where it is also out of place). According to this mentality, people are best served by mechanical systems that force them to conform to pressures of the system. Those who will not conform are left outside the system and thus are not served. At a recent visit to a California winery, I saw wine bottles fed into a conveyor belt system in which they were filled, labeled, and corked. Each bottle was shunted through the system in exactly the same way. Those not conforming to the system were rejected by it and seemed to be discarded.

Such a mechanized system in the name of ministry is not infrequently forced on those who cannot resist such a program—children and younger teens. However, when these young persons come of age, one thing many of them do is reject just such systems. This rejection appears to be one explanation for the dramatic dropout of older teens and young adults from the church, and for a growing number of persons who as "system misfits" are served by no ministry. On the other hand, the mechanization mentality seems to be one reason why the churches from their side seem unable to reach out to them through imaginative and innovative efforts. The old task of ministry was to serve the assembled; the new task of ministry is to assemble those to be served.

The task of leading persons to the kind of transformation called conversion is not a mechanized task and is not open to easy manipulation. In the face of the not-able-to-be-manipulated transformation called conversion, persons in ministry must stand in reverence and awe before the mystery of human freedom and the comparatively slow process of human development. Linear or unidimensional programs will not do, as Rahner reminds us in the following piece of pastoral wisdom.

> A pastoral approach which recognizes only one recipe for everything, which aims at opening every door with one single key, which thinks itself to be in possession of an Archimedean fulcrum from which it can proceed to move the whole world, is refuted by the simple ontological reflection that man is a plural being; that this plurality, despite the fact that man is also a unity,

is something that a man himself cannot get beyond; and that if the existential significance of this plurality is not to be, in practice, denied, there can be no one single point for him from which everything can be surveyed, everything worked out and everything directed. . . . The humility and patience which goes with plurality . . . belongs to the creaturely humility to be found in truly Christian pastoral work.[65]

Young adults are not going to respond to superficial bandwagon initiatives of spiritual hucksters. They want something better—and deserve something more. They are looking for the signs of transformation in the very persons and communities that would call them to transformation. Young adults, just like so many middle-aged and older adults, are looking for trustworthy guides and for communities that will keep faith with them. Ironically, there are many young adults who are truly unchurched and who are painfully conscious of this. These young people long to be part of a community of trustworthy persons willing to follow a step at a time Jesus' way. In their search for such a community some judge the trustworthiness of communities by their stance on social justice, Jesus' own standard. These young people are calling to the churches to be better, to become further liberated, to be zones that combine freedom and mutual direction, to be more given over to the service of one's sisters and brothers.

My second assertion is that *the evangelization demands that the churches first be converted to young adults.* People working with young adults are already discovering the ancient pastoral principle that has been recently rediscovered by those working with teens: Before these persons will be converted in a way that will lead them to stand within the community of the church, the church, or persons representing it, must first stand within their circle of experience. The church must be converted to them in its ministry to them. The matter of crossing over through love and understanding into the culture and individual experience of others is a topic treated extensively in the catechetical literature on evangelization that has been overlooked by so many current bandwagon evangelizers.

The matter is not difficult to comprehend. It is something every parent of a young child understands: a key part of the task of parenting involves a crossing-over into the world and experience of the child. Such a transformation is not automatic; it comes from decision and demands a change of life-style for the parents, as well as a careful attentiveness. The parent does not abdicate adulthood in this conversion to the child but rather extends and enriches maturity. I doubt that any work of nurture with another person can be successful without some sort of conversion to the experience of that person. Good therapists and counselors well understand this matter, which is a central one in the modern theory of catechesis/evangelization, as is evident in the literature of the last two Roman Synods.

There is a further dimension of this conversion of the church to young adults. It is this: Christian communities need young adults: their gifts, their questions and concerns, their insights and wisdom. Ironically, the young adults with the most to offer Christian communities are the ones who are most marginal in society. They bring to the churches their gift of marginality, their gift of not fitting in. Jesus himself consistently discovered the presence of God in the marginal persons of his time; he found the word of God spoken most loudly among them. The marginal ones were the ones who called forth a quality of Good News not possible among the comfortable and the well-settled.

A community wishing to be credible to young adults would best start by attending to the most marginalized among them: the divorced, the marginalized singles, the unskilled unemployed, the gays, those reentering society from prison, those searching for a simplified life-style, and so on. Without denying that Jesus-centered communities have something to offer such persons, I would stress that these edge-persons have much to give us and will call us to further transformations.

One of the great continuing dilemmas of the churches is that of effectively entering the lives of actual persons. In the person of Jesus we see most clearly that the law of salvation is Incarnation; it is God's way of leading persons to himself. The task that must continue to guide the churches is that of allowing God to become more deeply present in the midst of human life through our own presence to life. But that seems to be the very point where we balk. We do not balk at the possibility of meeting God; we balk at the possibility of meeting our fellowmen and women, and at the possibility that we will discover right there the astonishing presence of God.

Some Guidelines

Ministry to young adults as a focused pastoral area in the United States is in its infancy. Much more discussion of key issues needs to take place. I would suggest, however, some points for further reflection by those concerned with ministry to young adults, including the ministry of evangelization.

1. The research on the age period eighteen to thirty-five, especially Levinson's, suggests that religious questions are not the up-front concerns of persons during those years. Levinson's descriptions of the "Pulling Up Roots" stage (eighteen to twenty-three), of the "Getting Started" stage (twenty-three to twenty-eight), and of the "Age Thirty Transition" all suggest a preoccupation with personal developmental tasks not easy to negotiate in contemporary society. Note that I am not suggesting that religious concerns are not at the core of human existence. Religious concerns are always present and central, though not always in a self-conscious, reflexive way. However, if Levinson is correct, it may mean that most young adults need ministries of guidance, counsel, and healing, at least as their first concern, along with our ministry of religious meaning being given a distinct second place. My own work with college students suggests that many of them search for counsel and healing before they search for explicit religious meaning. Communities must be ready to offer guidance and healing to young adults who may not be interested right now in the ministry of the word or in the ministry of worship. Those ministries should continue to offer an open invitation to young people to enter in a full way the beloved community. We are called to open-handed ministry independent of the question of religious affiliation.

2. Young adults tend to be mobile. My hunch is that most highly mobile people have a special need to be welcomed and to be able to affiliate with communities in real but temporary ways. Any member of a vowed community can testify to the joy and comfort of being welcomed, when a traveler, into a community as a sister or a brother. I myself remember how impressed I was as a fourteen-year-old at the welcome I received by a community of Quakers at an Indian reservation in northern Maine—and by their exhortations that I visit "the brethren" in another community when I returned home. While

such invitations may not be possible today among Christians in our large churches, I suggest they be given more attention.

Some charismatic prayer groups have already established such a network of hospitality. At any rate, young adults tend to move naturally toward communities that extend a welcome. One such community is the Young Adult Network in San Francisco, with its marvelous Network Coffee House. The Network's basic stance is one of hospitality, and within that stance there are several levels of affiliation. In some local churches the sequence is reversed. The basic stance is one of first requiring full affiliation with too little attention to the matter of hospitality.

3. A key dilemma for ministry to young adults is that of finding trustworthy guides whose trustworthiness will be perceivable to young adults. Not everyone in a particular community has such a gift. Neither has every priest or person in formal ministry such a gift for ministry to young adults. Yet the gifts are there, present in each community, if it will also have the wisdom and sensitivity to discern them, call them forth, and develop them.

The sort of persons needed in this ministry are described in the following passage, in which Karl Rahner specifically writes about males and priests and which I would want to extend to any person ministering with young adults.

> We need to have, far more than perhaps we do have, the charismatic pastor, the man to whom Nicodemus can come in the night as he came to Jesus: the man in whose truly authentic religious existence even the skeptical man of today can believe, without getting the impression that it is a secondary, not personally authentic, product of tradition, a result of being entangled in the clerical office. Are we not often lacking in such pastors, men who are capable of being "prototypes" of religious existence in all its authenticity? Are there enough pastors who radiate the power to awaken others? How many priests are there who are brave enough to pray aloud, spontaneously, to speak of the more sublime things of the spiritual life; uninhibited enough to say anything spiritual outside the discharge of their office, in a fully personal way? Do we not get the impression here and there that recourse is had to official, organizational, sodality-type procedures because we dare not lay claim to any experience or success at the most important and most sublime level of real pastoral work . . . ?[66]

The qualities of trustworthiness and the ability to keep faith which Rahner describes here cannot be faked or slickly "promoted" among young adults. These qualities emerge from a quality of human existence.

4. A final guiding reflection fits in with the one above. The key to ministry of any kind with young adults lies within the young adults themselves. Young adults know the territory—the persons, the places, the issues, the feelings and hurts. Young adults need to be the chief ministers to other young adults. This is the principle guiding the work of Susan Klein among the young adults of San Antonio. In a series of carefully planned pastoral steps she has gathered a network of young adults who have a posture of care and service to other young people. Persons wishing to focus more clearly on this ministry would do well to examine the approach Susan Klein has used. My suspicion is that most successful ministries among young adults are in some sense peer ministries.

Conclusion

Alert readers will recognize that almost everything I have said about evangelization/ministry to young adults is true of ministry to any person. The gift that marginal young adults are giving to persons in ministry is a general raising of consciousness about principles of ministry that we have tended to overlook.

12

Spirituality for Young Adults

I would like to begin with the image of one of the ballet sequences in Verdi's opera *Aida*. In the Temple at Memphis, the priest dresses as a giant bird, say, an eagle, and does a ritual dance before the altar of the Egyptian God Phtah. The dance itself is one of dazzling beauty, as a man imitates this great bird—a fellow creature. With outstretched arms draped in feathers, the dancer in swooping gestures suggests the powerful flight, the effortless gliding, and the delicate landing of what could be an eagle.

What is striking in this ballet sequence is that a creature is praising God through imitating the movement, the creatureliness of another creature. Only a human is endowed with the creative capacity to imitate, in such uncanny mimicry, the subtleties in the movements of a great winged creature. The underlying sense of the dance is, first, that God is praised in the creatureliness of his creatures, in the "birdliness" of the bird. But in a second sense, God is doubly praised when man represents the loveliness of the creature to God. Human creativity is the great act of worship.

In addition to the obvious significance of this ballet in *Aida*, what struck me powerfully, the way insight comes with special force through art, was that men and women themselves, as persons living out their humanity, are the great hymns of praise to God. The greatest song of praise to God is the humanliness of women and men.

To accept one's life-project of being a human person, to grow in one's humanity, to move toward being more of a person—this is the great task of life. And this is the great act of worship, to become the full creature God has called us to be. If the mimicry of the priest in *Aida* is an achievement, that achievement pales before the achievement of growing into more of a human person.[67]

That is where I would like to begin my reflections on the spirituality of young adults: With the great task we are all faced with of growing in our humanity, that is, in our fidelity to the possibilities of full humanness that God has placed within each of us. Will we dance before the Lord, will our spirits open out to their full capacity following the whisperings of God within us? And just what does that mean, anyway, to grow in our humanity?

I believe that we must think hard about spirituality, that is, about the direction of our lives as living spirits, as embodied spirits. To me this is the great question of each person's life: In what direction should I as this particular human person tend? That question goes beyond asking what career I should choose or even what partner I should choose. The question of spirituality is related to career and partner, but beyond even those important matters, it is rooted in our values, in what we stand for, in the kind of "feel" people who know us get from us. Spirituality, in the sense I am using it, refers to the thrust of one's human spirit. It is not so much concerned with the style of one's prayer as it is with what people will think we stood for when they themselves stand at our coffin.

Why should I want to deal with this topic, when most of the literature about young adults speaks of their developmental stages, of their various tasks: their career tasks, their psychological tasks, and their interpersonal tasks? The reason is that after teaching hundreds of young people in their twenties over the past several years, I see considerable confusion about what those things are that a human being should attend to and what matters are worth investing one's life in. Worse still, among some I find *no confusion*, but rather unspoken and unexamined presuppositions about the matters and values that should orient a human existence. So many young people I have met have been put to sleep, anesthetized, at least in their consciousness, not by coke, pot, heroin, alcohol, but by media hype, by slogans, by the stock situations of evening TV comedy and afternoon melodrama. They do not actually stand for anything. So in my teaching I find the only way of getting behind these taken-for-granteds is by asking, to the point of annoyance: What do you stand for? In what direction does your human spirit tend? What is worth living for? What is worth dying for? What kind of person do you want to be at forty? What is in your heart? At your death, what do you want to be able to say was not negotiable in your life? (Will it be, "I pursued quality: I bought only Sony and Nikon?")

At this point someone could easily ask: Why pick on young adults? Do not a considerable number of older adults show much confusion about which matters are worthwhile? Why pick on us? And I agree. Mature adults need to be confronted with questions of their spirituality also. However, the sharp importance of these questions in young adults lies in their beginning to establish a life structure and a life-style.[68] Life structure and life-style are the vehicles by which a spirituality moves. They embody a spirituality. It is life structure and life-style that carry an emerging spirituality into later life.[69] Ultimately, the mindlessness of youth leads to the mindlessness of old age. Listen to the following passage from Ronald Blythe's book about old age, *The View in Winter*, and note its connection with patterns established in youth.

> Many old people reduce life to such trifling routines that they cause the rest of us to turn away in revulsion. Sometimes we should say to them, "How can you expect us to be interested in this minimal you, with your mean days and little grumbles?" This slide into purposelessness must not be confused with the ability of the old not to take life all that seriously, for this has its virtues and assets. To appreciate the transience of all things is one matter, to narrow the last years—and they can be numerous—down to a dreary thread is another. One of the most dreadful sights in the country of the old is that of the long rows of women playing the Las Vegas slot machines. Had Dante heard of it he would have cleared a space for it in Hell. It is symbolic of that specially self-indulgent mindlessness of old age which is its most intolerable aspect.[70]

This passage can easily be transposed to address a mindlessness at any age. Young adulthood is the time when one determines what things to pay attention to, what matters will be worth the expenditure of money, time, and energy. Basic decisions made now will determine whether at mid-life one's vision is limited to the next patch of crab grass on the front lawn or the next buy-of-a-lifetime at the local discount store.[71]

As a kind of preface to some directions for the spirit life of young adults, I wish to highlight an important idea of psychologist Erik Erikson dealing with the question of growth throughout the life cycle. Erikson says, ". . . crisis at any age does not necessarily mean a threat or a catastrophe but rather a turning point, a crucial period of increased vulnerability and heightened potential."[72] What seems to happen throughout life is that when a new stage of growth is called for, one faces a question of going forward or backward, that is, of facing the new stage and the transformations it calls for or of "copping out." If one "cops out" one does not develop the virtue that will result if one faces up to and goes through the crisis. For example, in adolescence the crisis/challenge is to forge one's identity, one's sense of oneself, one's uniqueness. The resulting virtue is fidelity, meaning that a person has a standpoint and a resulting believability. Yet if the person backs away from this challenge, he or she can grow up having no standpoint, standing for nothing, a reed shaken in the wind.[73] You go to poke the person to see if she or he is real, and you find you have stuck your finger in pudding. Or worse still, the person solves the struggle to stand for something with the pseudo-solution of adopting quick but rigid positions devoid of ambiguity or questions. This is quite a price to pay for certitude, but it is paid willingly so one's head can go back to sleep.[74]

According to Erikson, the life stages and the life tasks connected with the stages are all themselves interrelated. Thus in order to move on to the development of intimacy, which Erikson says is a key task of early adulthood, one must first have come to grips with identity and its accompanying virtue of fidelity.[75] Intimacy without fidelity is a sham intimacy. The young adults I have met are not for the most part afraid of intimacy; they are afraid of intimacy without fidelity. It is the fidelity half of intimacy, or the lack of it, that is causing so much pain in the lives of many young adults I know. The epidemic afflicting many of these young people is the epidemic of betrayal, of having given oneself and then realizing one has been used and discarded. Apparently many young adults are good at taking off their clothes; not so many are as good at cherishing the possibilities of another human spirit.

What then is the specific advice I would give for the spirits of young adults, who have the courage to work at their life-project of becoming more human? I suggest three qualities of the spirituality of young adults. Each quality will be developed in the face of the temptation to develop an exactly opposite trait or quality. What I am suggesting is a spirituality of connectedness; a spirituality of gradualness or patience; and a spirituality of simplicity.

1. A Spirituality of Connectedness

By connectedness, I mean obviously and first of all, the sort of connectedness with significant others that helps us be human beings. I mean first the kind of connectedness anyone finds in a good friendship, that is, significant sharing of selves in an ambience of loyalty and fidelity. I have been telling the students in my marriage class that if I could say one thing to help young people prepare for marriage, I would not talk about marriage at all but about friendship. Married friendship, it seems to me, is both prepared for and made understandable by other, more ordinary friendships. Yet so many of the young adults I meet see marriage in discontinuity with their other friendships; they do not think of husband or wife in terms of friendship. They do not think: This is the person with whom I have achieved the kind of friendship I can call husband or wife.

The condition of disconnectedness or of very superficial connectedness is suggested by Philip Levine in his poem, "Belle Isle, 1949."

> We stripped in the first warm spring night
> and ran down into the Detroit River
> to baptize ourselves in the brine
> of car parts, dead fish, stolen bicycles,
> melted snow. I remember going under
> hand in hand with a Polish highschool girl
> I'd never seen before, and the cries
> our breath made caught at the same time
> on the cold, and rising through the layers
> of darkness into the final moonless atmosphere
> that was this world, the girl breaking
> the surface after me and swimming out
> on the starless waters towards the lights

of Jefferson Ave. and the stacks
of the old stove factory unwinking.
Turning at last to see no island at all
but a perfect calm dark as far
as there was sight, and then a light
and another riding low out ahead
to bring us home, ore boats maybe, or smokers
walking alone. Back panting
to the gray coarse beach we didn't dare
fall on, the damp piles of clothes,
and dressing side by side in silence
to go back where we came from.

This is the kind of disconnection we are called to move from.

However a spirituality of connectedness goes far beyond the connectedness of even good friends. If our connectedness stays at only this level then we have understood only a small part of human reality. The connectedness of friendship is a personal connectedness; it connects us in a household or neighborhood sense. Beyond the neighborhood, however, is the section or area, and beyond that the city or town, the county, the state, the geographical region, the nation, the continent, the hemisphere, *the world*. The world is the sphere of very serious but hidden connectedness. So many young adults I meet have opted out, possibly not theoretically but functionally, of their global connectedness. Their attention is fixed at the level of the household or possibly the neighborhood. One can find out what gets one's attention by seeing how (or even whether) one reads the newspaper. To read only the sports page, or only the ads, or only the news classified as bizarre or gossip is to be disconnected in a global sense.

Let me put it this way. In the 1950s Maryknoll Father James Keller founded a movement he called the Christophers. It had the goal of alerting each person to the difference she or he could make in her or his immediate surroundings. The motto of the Christophers was and still is: You can change the world. Not correctly understood that motto can be dangerous. It can rest on a fundamental misunderstanding of the complexity of the world. It can encourage persons to go their own personal way of goodness, leaving the big social movements and the true power in the world in the hands of the multidegreed ignoramuses and the well-heeled and well-perfumed masters of oppression.

You cannot change the world by yourself. Those with power want you to think you can. They will let you go your ineffectual way with their blessing. You can be a *sign* to others of the possibilities of goodness in an individual life, but to foster institutionalized goodness or to counter institutionalized evil one must band with properly intentioned and competent persons and work together for significant change. We cannot allow our efforts to follow the gospel to become fixated at the level of helping people onto buses, tipping our hats, or even giving kind, affirming words. All that is too easy. The spirituality I suggest is one that says: You can change the world if you are willing to abandon a backyard mentality and enter the world by starting to pay attention to the wider issues and by networking with persons of similar vision.[76]

I have been trying to find an image to capture the privatized world of some young adults, and there is one that does this well. It is the image of the van. What does the van represent? It represents a search for intimacy. The van's specialness is not found in its motor but in its interior—the custom interior. The ones I have seen are carpeted two ways: floors, walls, ceilings done in broadloom; and the ensemble carpeted in quadraphonic sound. The van is a nest on wheels; it is set up for a small, intimate number, usually two—the couple. The silvered windows symbolize this intimacy and protectedness from the outside world. In a van you can see out but "they" cannot see in.

The van represents other dimensions of a young adult's life too, such as the desire for change and adventure. In a van the possibilities are endless. On a weekend this van can go anywhere. Hidden here is a kind of nonresponsibility. This van *can* go anywhere. We are not tied down. *Our* nest has wheels. Another dimension suggested by the van is the search for sexual fulfillment. For many young people the van is a statement of sexual freedom, as can be seen on some of the bumper signs: "If this van's rockin', don't bother knockin' "; or, "Don't laugh: your daughter might be in here."

If it is true that the van represents a private world, a closed, hidden environment, and a chance to look out on life without getting involved, then it represents also the sorts of attitudes and life-styles we must move away from if we are to espouse a life that looks to wider human connectedness—that moves beyond the fantasies of childhood and adolescence to a growing sense of human responsibility.

2. A Spirituality of Gradualness and Patience

Understanding the gradualness of human growth is a matter I judge to be of special importance in any human, Christian life. It is an understanding that has become central to me through my own concern with teens, who are very much in process and painfully aware of it. However, as I have been able to meet and interact with persons in other stages in the life cycle I have come to see to what extent patience and an acceptance of gradualness are keys to any human growth. As human persons, we are incomplete, works-of-art-in-process. The irony of the human condition is that a realistic acceptance of this incompleteness is the first step toward getting seriously involved in our human project. Patience with oneself is a step toward claiming one's uniqueness and individuality. It takes great courage for any person to embrace his or her incompleteness and to move forward with one's own possibilities a step at a time.[77]

What are the implications of a spirituality of patience and gradualness? Let me cite two out of possible dozens. The first is in the matter of sexuality. In my classes at St. John's University in New York, I explain this matter of incompleteness with great care and then apply it to sexuality. One does not move to sexual maturity in one great bound at puberty. The move to sexual potency is fairly quick, but the move to maturity as a sexual person is gradual. To become more tender as one ages, to become more *true* in one's embodiment or physical expression of feeling, to become sexually more trustworthy, to grow in one's ability to be comfortable with a range of emotional responses—these are all tasks that take time and attention, tasks affected by the quality of our judgment, good or bad.[78]

It must be said baldly that to grow in any skill or other area of life means growing by means of error, just as truth emerges from doubt. At least we can grow by means of our halting, stumbling progress. I would rather have made sexual mistakes and have grown thereby than to have remained a sexual infant because I walled myself in sexually, never left the house, and consequently never made a mistake. (Like Chance the Gardener in *Being There*.) When I have reflected with young people along these lines, again and again different persons have expressed relief at recognizing a common-sense truth which they had rarely or never heard expressed before. The surest way to sexual folly is to try to accomplish everything at once and to hold oneself to an ideal of perfection and completeness not possible to a human being.

We need a spirituality of gradualness also in our search for a life-defining heterosexual friend, our intimate-friend-for-life, our marriage friend. If you listen to persons tell their stories, most do not find immediately their marriage-friend. Most undergo many heterosexual encounters, some of which become true friendships, before they find and enter the life-defining friendship. To be gradual in this realm, to be *not* hyper, to be calm, to focus instead on being true to one's self is a great preparation for meeting or for becoming a life-defining friend.

It seems to me that for a young adult who is single and hoping to marry, part of one's growth lies in learning to tolerate loneliness and aloneness. Aloneness is important for developing a depth of life and for being in touch with one's uniqueness. Loneliness is a condition of life that erupts when one's spirit aches in reaching out for intimacy. Loneliness, like other forms of suffering, is unavoidable for most persons. It is part of the human condition. My hunch is that for many young people, loneliness sets them into a panic of scrambling headlong for any relationship, even a disastrous one. Here we need to remember that relationships themselves have about them a gradualness and the search for the right kinds of relationships must also be characterized by patience or a toleration for one step at a time.

The patience of young adults can be a gift to the rest of the human community. According to recent studies, young people in their twenties are going through a major life shift or transition. They are in process, so much so that change seems to be a key dynamic of their lives.[79] What the young people I know do for me is remind me that process and change are the law of all life. These young people are in such a period of questioning that they remind me—even allow me—to be in touch with my own questions. Some older people like to posture a neat stability and fixity which is actually a cosmetic stability, an illusion of stability.

3. A Spirituality of Simplicity

According to Rahner, the key to the human is freedom. What fosters human freedom is what fosters the human. Moral action becomes more authentically human the more it is based on human freedom. However, today all of us are so open to manipulation, especially by the media, that if we are to be free in ourselves, we have to struggle toward it. We have to pursue a simple life-style, a life-style that operates out of an understanding of what we do not need, rather than one that operates out of fantasies of all the things we could have or should have.

We are all enduring an assault on our senses which overwhelms us when we are not even aware of it. There is more danger, more poison in the things we see and hear than in the things we drink and eat. Two recent films dealt with sensory overload. The first, *All That Jazz*, depicts the manic, frantic life of a choreographer whose days and nights are so filled with sensory overload that he is ultimately destroyed. I do not recommend the film, which in itself is an assault on the senses that can put the viewer into a kind of panic. The other film, *Being There*, is about a man whose total view of reality comes from TV, and we soon find we are dealing with a walking vegetable, with zero emotional response and "rice pudding between his ears."

What frightens me about the spirituality of so many adults in their forties and fifties is that their horizon is limited to the next thing they will buy. Listen to the casual conversation of many persons of this age, and what do you find fills that conversation: incessant talk about money and goods. They are consumed by a kind of consumer lust. They are possessed by their possessions.[80] If we do not want to end up in mid-life chattering endlessly about our hard-earned money, if we do not want our imaginations fixated at the level of our next fantasy of the buy of a lifetime, then we must pursue a more simple life-style. We must acknowledge the things we do not need and the things we do not want; the things we do not need to eat; the kind of violence we will not watch and the sort of aural porn we will not listen to.[81]

We may not all be able to subscribe to the following words of Dorothy Day, because they are radical; but listen to them and substitute the word simplicity for poverty, if poverty is a word too strong for you.

> Poverty is a very mysterious thing. We need to be always writing and thinking about it. And of course, striving for it. It would seem strange that we must strive to be poor, to remain poor. "Just give me a chance," I can hear people say, "Just let me get my debts paid. Just let me get a few of the things I need and then I'll begin to think of poverty and its pleasures. Meanwhile I've had nothing but." I am convinced that if we had an understanding and a love of poverty we would begin to be as free and joyous as St. Francis, who had a passion for Lady Poverty, and lives on with us in joyous poverty through all the centuries since his death.[82]

Dorothy Day gives us here an inkling of the challenge of simplicity and its joys.

These then are my suggestions for a spirituality suited to a particular time of one's life. What is it like to be young and to have reached a point in your life when you can make decisions for yourself, when you can begin to establish yourself in your own living space, "on your own," when you can use your own financial resources in the way you want, when the days of handouts from parents are over? You have more control, more power. What is it like? You can tell me what it feels like better than I can tell you. What I can say about this period is that like every period of our lives it has its own special temptation. The temptation is to become concerned only with oneself; to indulge all the fantasies of *having* that have crept into your consciousness after years of having your wants manipulated by the marketeers; to turn inward and to ignore life at the level of the race, ignore it at the level of the questions facing the international community, ignore one's own place in being one, single, alert, aroused consciousness of the broad questions of the human species. The temptation is to retreat to the nest, to the cleverly produced mobile womb, the van, or to the pseudo-social, pseudo-intimate world of the beer bash at Cleo's, of the roller disco, of flag-waving because "our" team beat the Russians at hockey.[83]

What am I saying, I who begin on the one hand by speaking of dancing before the Lord, an image of joy and enlivened-ness, and end with a slur at disco, lively, swinging modern dance? Am I serious? Am I not contradicting myself? No. I am suggesting the danger of reducing the scope of our humanness to the mindless and the superficial and the pseudo. I am pointing out the danger of being manipulated, of being had by the forces in our society that point out the easy, soft, half-asleep road. I am pointing instead to the restlessness that is a sign of life. I am pointing to the kinds of concerns that can define a human life in such a way that at forty-five one's vision will not be restricted to the next patch of crab grass that must be dug out of the lawn or to the next buy-of-a-lifetime to pop up in the newspaper ads. Ultimately I am pointing to the one who danced before God most beautifully, most lithely, most courageously on the side of his sisters and brothers, showing them the true contours and the true possibilities of life on this earth: Jesus. It is his kind of living spirit I have been proposing.

References

¹ The most comprehensive quasi-official statement on youth ministry for Catholics is "A Vision of Youth Ministry," a 12-page document published by the Department of Education at the U.S. Catholic Conference in Washington, after a 15-month period of consultation and revision. See "A Vision of Youth Ministry" (Washington: USCC, 1976).

² The recent survey of parish catechetical programs, conducted by Rev. Eugene Hemrick of the U.S. Catholic Conference in conjunction with the Boys Town Center for the Study of Youth Development, shows that the majority of Catholic parishes have not begun to implement a new vision of youth ministry. See A National Inventory of Parish Catechetical Programs (Washington: U.S. Catholic Conference, 1978), especially pp. 37–42, 54. For a summary of this report, see "Parish Catechetical Personnel and Programs," Origins 8:15 (Sept. 28, 1978), pp. 225–234.

³ The dropout rate was documented in a study of catechetical programs done in 1976 by the Boys Town Center in cooperation with the U.S. Catholic Conference. See Wilfrid H. Paradis and Andrew D. Thompson, Where Are the 6.6 Million? (Washington: USCC, 1976).

⁴ It is possible that more writing and publishing has been done by Catholics than by Protestants, with the exception of the books by Merton Strommen. One of the most valuable recent contributions by Catholics is a volume that, unfortunately, may be overlooked, since it is published in the format of a journal and by a publisher not tied to a distribution network. The book is Catechesis: Realities and Visions, the compilation of papers given between March 13–16, 1977, at the Symposium on the Catechesis of Children and Youth held at Marriottsville, Md., sponsored by the USCC Department of Education. See Berard L. Marthaler and Marianne Sawicki, eds., Catechesis: Realities and Visions (Washington: USCC, 1977).

⁵ This catechetical renewal, and its character of reclaiming a fuller sense of the tradition of leading persons to a deeper faith, is not always attended to by persons examining the theory of religious education-Christian education. Thus a recent review of the approaches to religious education of James Michael Lee and John Westerhoff deals with their thought totally outside of catechetical categories. Yet, Westerhoff himself affirms that

Roman Catholic catechetical theory is a valid context within which to understand his own approach. See Didier Piveteau and James Dillon, "Two Scholarly Views on Religious Education: Lee and Westerhoff," *Lumen Vitae* 32:1 (1977), pp. 7–44; and, John Westerhoff, "A Call to Catechesis," *Living Light* 14:3 (1977), pp. 354–358.

⁶ In one of its published forms this directory appears with notes and commentary by Berard Marthaler. Marthaler's work gives the reader a good sense of the scope of the catechetical renewal among Catholics. See Berard L. Marthaler, *Catechetics in Context* (Huntington, Ind.: Our Sunday Visitor Press, 1973).

⁷ D. S. Amalorpavadass, "Nature, Purpose, and Process of Catechesis within the Pastoral Activity of the Church," in William Tobin, ed., *International Catechetical Congress: Selected Documentation* (Washington: USCC, 1972), pp. 39–59. Amalorpavadass' talk appeared in 1972 in a slightly revised version but under a different title. See D. S. Amalorpavadass, "Catechesis as a Pastoral Task of the Church," *Lumen Vitae* 27 (1972), pp. 259–280.

⁸ I have tried to suggest a reason for what could be called a growing convergence of ministries, especially in the Catholic Church. See "Youth Ministry: An Overview," in Michael Warren, ed., *Youth Ministry: A Book of Readings* (N.Y.: Paulist Press, 1977), pp. 3–9.

⁹ The issue of the relationship between education and ministry has been of considerably more importance to me than to many colleagues in religious education. Only time will reveal the long-term significance of the distinction. For a more in-depth treatment, see Michael Warren, "A Framework for Catholic Education: Opportunities for the Future," in Durka and Smith, eds., *Emerging Issues in Religious Education* (N.Y.: Paulist Press, 1976), pp. 99–113.

¹⁰ Marthaler and Sawicki suggest that the best sign of successful catechesis may well be "replication of ministry" or the response of engaging in ministry. For their valuable comments on this issue, see "No Final Word," in *Catechesis: Realities and Visions*, pp. 180–188.

¹¹ See various articles in the section on leadership development in the following work: Michael Warren, ed., *Resources for Youth Ministry* (N.Y.: Paulist Press, 1978), pp. 5–16; 45–78; 110–167.

¹² See Liz Harris, "Persons in Need of Supervision," *The New Yorker* (Aug. 14, 1978), pp. 55–89. Also see two works by Gisela Konopka dealing with adolescent girls: *The Adolescent Girl in Conflict* (Englewood Cliffs, NJ: Prentice-Hall, 1966) and *Young Girls: A Portrait of Adolescence* (Prentice-Hall, 1976).

¹³ See James Coleman, ed., *Youth: Transition to Adulthood* (Chicago: University of Chicago Press, 1974).

¹⁴ D. S. Amalorpavadass, "Theory of Evangelization," in Joseph Pathrapankal, ed., *Service and Salvation* (Bangalore, India: Theological Publications, 1973), pp. 37–38.

[15] William F. Lynch, *Images of Faith: An Exploration of the Ironic Imagination* (Notre Dame, Ind.: Univ. of Notre Dame Press, 1973), p. 23.

[16] *Living Light* 10:4: pp. 498–499.

[17] Marc Oraison, *Love or Constraint* (N.Y.: Paulist Press, 1961), p. 72.

[18] Rosemary Haughton, "Family Spirituality: A Kind of Joy." *New Catholic World* (March 1976), pp. 80–84.

[19] Karl Rahner, *Theological Investigations*, v. 7, "On Truthfulness," (N.Y.: Herder and Herder, 1971), pp. 252–253.

[20] See Van C. Kussrow, "Fantasy, Imagination, and Liturgy," *Liturgy* 24:1 (Jan.-Feb. 1979), p. 6.

[21] Susanne K. Langer, *Philosophy in a New Key: A Study in the Symbolism of Reason, Rite and Art* (Cambridge, Mass.: Harvard Univ. Press, 1957), p. 45.

[22] Henri J. M. Nouwen, "More People, More Love." *National Catholic Reporter* (Oct. 13, 1975), p. 14.

[23] Donald Evans, *Struggle and Fulfillment: The Inner Dynamics of Religion and Morality* (Cleveland: Collins Publishers, 1979), p. 134.

[24] Andrew Kopkind, "The Dialectic of Disco." *The Village Voice* (Feb. 12, 1979), p. 11.

[25] My own attempts to interpret this situation and to point to new directions can be found in: M. Warren, *A Future for Youth Catechesis* (N.Y.: Paulist Press, 1975), and in "New Directions," pp. 5–17 and "Evangelization of Youth," pp. 47–57 of M. Warren, ed., *Youth Ministry: A Book of Readings* (N.Y.: Paulist Press, 1977).

[26] For a summary of this sort of thinking see, *A Vision of Youth Ministry* (Washington: USCC, 1976).

[27] See Merton Strommen, *Five Cries of Youth* (N.Y.: Harper & Row, 1974), especially pp. 12–32 and 112–126. Also, William S. Starr, "Young Life Focus: Friendship," in M. Warren, ed., *Resources for Youth Ministry*, pp. 59–65.

[28] This way of relating the coherence of communities to common understandings, common judgments, and common commitments is a central thesis in the thought of Bernard Lonergan. It is also a common assumption in the literature of the sociology of knowledge. See Bernard Lonergan, *Collection:* (N.Y.: Herder and Herder, 1967), p. 245.

[29] In making this statement I am not ignoring the 1977 Roman synod, which dealt with catechesis, particularly in its mission to children and youth. Preparation by the U.S. delegation of bishops and their advisors did set in motion an increased dialogue about youth catechesis between 1977 and 1979. Such dialogue was heightened by the work of preparing the various drafts of the National Catechetical Directory, finally published in 1979 as *Sharing the Light of Faith.*

However, these discussions do not seem to have given much guidance to youth work at local levels across the nation. Even the papers at the 1977

Symposium on the Catechesis of Children and Youth, held in preparation for the synod, are for the most part curiously devoid of catechetical principles for guiding efforts at catechizing youth outside the schools. With a few exceptions, which include the valuable commentary to the published papers, most of the material talks around catechesis. See Berard Marthaler and Marianne Sawicki, ed., *Catechesis: Realities and Visions.*

[30] Pope John Paul II, *Catechesi Tradendae*, Origins 9:21 (Nov. 8, 1979), pp. 329, 331–348. The paragraph cited here appears on page 336 of the *Origins* edition.

[31] Although the description of evangelization here is accurate, one should note that since the 1974 Roman synod dealing with evangelization, the word has been increasingly used in two senses: in the specialized sense of its use in this paragraph and in a general sense that equates evangelization with the ministry of the word. Pope Paul VI's apostolic exhortation on evangelization, *Evangelii Nuntiandi*, uses the word in both its particular and general senses, as does the more recent *Catechesi Tradendae*. To avoid confusion, persons serious about the nuanced understanding of catechetical matters must pay attention to the context in which evangelization is used. For background on the specialized meaning of evangelization, see M. Warren, "Evangelization: A Catechetical Concern," *Living Light* 10:4 (1973), pp. 487–496.

[32] The need for imagination and boldness in pastoral ministry has been highlighted in essays written in the past decade by Rahner and Lonergan. I think it would be accurate to say that developments in youth ministry of the past 10 years exemplify the very kind of thoughtful and imaginative planning called for by Lonergan and Rahner. However, these past accomplishments now need to be carried to another level if youth catechesis is to move forward. See Bernard Lonergan, "The Response of the Jesuit as Priest and Apostle in the Modern World," in *A Second Collection* (Philadelphia: Westminster Press, 1974), pp. 165–187; and Karl Rahner, "Do Not Stifle the Spirit," in *Theological Investigations*, vol. 8 (N.Y.: Herder and Herder, 1971), pp. 72–87.

[33] Although the precise language used here does not dominate catechetical literature, the ideas behind the language do dominate. Documenting this shift during the past twenty years would make a fascinating and instructive study. The subject-object distinction is a commonplace in current philosophy and theology. (See Lonergan, "The Subject," in *A Second Collection*, pp. 69–99). My own use of the term is influenced by Rahner's in such essays as, "Theology and Anthropology," *Theological Investigations*, vol. 9 (N.Y.: Herder and Herder, 1972), pp. 28–45.

[34] See "The Catechetical Presupposition," in *Future for Youth Catechesis*, pp. 19–28.

[35] See Walter Kasper, "Christian Humanism," in James M. Robinson, *Religion and the Humanizing of Man* (Waterloo, Ont.: Council on the Study of Religion, 1972), pp. 20–34.

[36] See Charles Davis, "Religion and the Sense of the Sacred," Catholic Theological Society of America Proceedings 31 (1976), pp. 87–105. This piece is an example of the sort of wide-angle focus we need. Davis is concerned with the images that dominate the lives of persons today and ultimately shape their world of meaning. One of his claims here is that some of the images that are supposed to orient the lives of Christians are no longer able to do so in the face of the challenges offered by logical, mechanistic secularity. What Davis is exploring is the key issue of the orientation of one's human spirit. For a related article but with a somewhat different focus, see Michael Novak, "The Unawareness of God," in Joseph P. Whalen, ed., The God Experience (N.Y.: Newman, 1971), pp. 6–25.

[37] See Pedro Arrupe, "Catechesis and Inculturation," Lumen Vitae 33:1 (1978), pp. 45–50.

[38] See Catechesi Tradendae, par. 59.

[39] This matter of a catechetical structure that tends to collapse at about age 12 has not been given anywhere near the attention it deserves. Gabriel Moran deals with it in his writings from an education-in-religion standpoint. Another good treatment is Kevin Coughlin, "Motivating Adults for Religious Education," Living Light 13:2 (1976), pp. 269–298. A more recent and important approach to the problem of terminal catechesis is Julia Ann Upton, "A Solution to the Infant Baptism Problem," Living Light 16:4 (1979), pp. 484–496.

[40] When I search for a "rule-of-thumb" indicator of the adequacy or inadequacy of any particular program of youth catechesis, I find the best indicator of a sound program in its celebrative character. A youth catechetical program that has a good celebrative character tends to have a sound catechetical character. On the other hand, a program that ignores the celebrative for an overconceptual focus tends to be catechetically inadequate.

[41] See Nancy Hennessy Cooney, "Deciding for Yourself, Not by Yourself: A Christian Sex Education Program for Junior High Youth and Their Parents," PACE 6 (1975): Issues, Section G. See also her recent book for teens, Sex, Sexuality and You (Dubuque, Iowa: W. C. Brown, 1980).

[42] According to Joseph F. Kett, the trivialization of the period of youth is not just a present possibility but a past actuality. His history of adolescence in the United States pays considerable attention to this trivialization. For instance,

> The difference between the early and late 19th century lay not merely in the extension of ecclesiastical control over the spare-time activities of youth but in the increasing erosion of the principle of voluntary association by youth. The young men's societies of the 17th through early 19th centuries had been organized by young men themselves; the young people's movement of the 1880's and 1890's, in contrast consisted entirely of adult-sponsored youth organizations. . . .

Christian youth organizations of the late 19th century downgraded not only voluntarism but intellectuality and spirituality as well. One sign of the direction was the preference of leaders of the young people's movement for "training" rather than "edification." To train youth for church work became a principle slogan of individuals like Francis E. Clark, but neither Clark nor the other leaders were able to define what role in the church young people were to be trained for. Clark offered a list of vapid possibilities: "training in public prayer and confession of the very simplest yet sincerest sort; training in preparation for the prayer-meeting committee; training in temperance and missionary zeal and different sorts of Sunday school work." Even when spokesmen for the young people's movement outlined specific goals, they were so general as to be meaningless (e.g., the immediate conversion of the world) or so trivial as to be ludicrous (e.g., running errands for the pastor).

Joseph F. Kett, *Rites of Passage: Adolescence in America, 1790 to the Present* (N.Y.: Basic Books, 1977), p. 194. See also pp. 189–211, esp. p. 210 and pp. 215–272.

[43] These ideals can be found in USCC Department of Education, *A Vision of Youth Ministry* (Washington: USCC, 1976).

[44] This conviction is a theme in both *Bridging the Gap* (Minneapolis: Augsburg Publishing, 1973) and *Five Cries of Youth.*

[45] The matter of adjudicated youth (youth put in secure facilities for commiting acts not crimes and for which no adult could be locked up) needs much more attention, even considering the significant attention it has gotten over the past five years. For some valuable information, see Liz Harris, "A Reporter at Large: Persons in Need of Supervision," *The New Yorker* (August 14, 1978), pp. 55–89. Also, Committee of the Judiciary, *Hearing before the Subcommittee to Investigate Juvenile Delinquency.* Ninety-fifth Congress, First Session, on S. 1021 and S. 1218 (Apr. 27, 1977) (Washington: U.S. Gov't Printing Office, 1978) and *Juvenile Justice Amendments of 1977:* Report of the Committee on the Judiciary, U.S. Senate on S. 1021 (95th Congress, 1st Session, Report #95–165) (Washington: U.S. Gov't Printing Office, 1977).

[46] This issue appears regularly in the popular press, reflecting current alarm over teenage pregnancies and also reflecting what is in fact a political struggle over who will have the chief voice in directing teens. For a valuable commentary, see Margaret O'Brien Steinfels, "Beyond the Medical Solution," *Commonweal* (May 23, 1980), pp. 310–312.

[47] See Ellen Goodman, "What They're Selling, Parents Aren't Buying," *Washington Post* (Oct. 14, 1980). Goodman's position in this editorial is one of a number of similar statements from articulate feminists.

[48] See some of the remarkable articles dealing with the teen market that regularly appear in the trade journals of the advertising industry: George P.

Moschis and Roy L. Moore, "Decision-Making Among the Young: A Socialization Perspective," *Journal of Consumer Research* 6 (Sept. 1979), pp. 101–112; Gerald J. Gorn and Marvin E. Goldberg, "The Impact of Television Advertising on Children from Low Income Families," *Journal of Consumer Research* 4 (Sept. 1977), pp. 86–88; George W. Schiele, "Reaching Teens with Same Message, *Advertising Age* (February 26, 1979), pp. 24–26, 29; George P. Moschis, "Teenagers' Response to Retailing Stimuli," *Journal of Retailing* 54:4 (Winter 1978), pp. 80–93; Ronald W. Stampfl, George Moschis, and Joseph T. Lawton, "Consumer Education and the Pre-School Child," *Journal of Consumer Affairs*, 12:1 (Summer 1978), pp. 12–29.

[49] I am calling here for what Paulo Freire terms "the critically transitive consciousness," a consciousness that sees beneath the surface in interpreting problems. Freire writes,

> The critically transitive consciousness is characterized by depth in the interpretation of problems; by the substitution of causal principles for magical explanations; by the testing of one's 'findings' and by openness to revision; by the attempt to avoid distortion when perceiving problems and to avoid preconceived notions when analyzing them; by refusing to transfer responsibility; by rejecting passive positions; by soundness of argumentation; by the practice of dialogue rather than polemics; by receptivity to the new for reasons beyond novelty and by the good sense not to reject the old just because it is old — by accepting what is valid in both old and new.

Paulo Freire, *Education for Critical Consciousness* (N.Y.: Seabury Press, 1973), pp. 18–19.

[50] The terminology of first and second naivete is that of Paul Ricoeur, but I am clearly using "second naivete" in a way quite different from his. For Ricoeur, second naivete is critical thought. I use the term to suggest a second level of unawareness. See Paul Ricoeur, *The Symbolism of Evil* (N.Y.: Harper & Row, 1967), pp. 347–357.

[51] C. Ellis Nelson puts this matter lucidly in *Where Faith Begins:*

> After seeing that the group of believers is the unit with which we must work, we must then see that whatever is done or said, or not done or said, *is* teaching. There is no such thing as postponing the solution to a problem. The decision to postpone is a decision; it teaches that the issue is too hot to handle, that such issues are not appropriate for the church, or that the tactic of postponement is more important at this point than a resolution to settle the matter. People learn from the way events are handled. There is no neutrality. If a congregation attempts to be neutral, it teaches that on the issues at hand it can't make up its mind, it is fearful of the result of a decision, or it is confused about how to proceed. There is no avoidance of an issue. Not to see an issue is to teach that Christians

do not see issues. Christians who avoid problems in social ethics—such as involvement in racial relations, war, or the distribution of wealth—are saying that the Christian faith does not operate in these areas.

C. Ellis Nelson, *Where Faith Begins* (Atlanta: John Knox Press, 1967), pp. 184–185.

[52] Paulo Freire uses the term "submerged" to describe the lack of awareness I here have in mind.

> Men (*sic*) submerged in the historical process are characterized by a state I have described as "semiintransitivity of consciousness." . . . Men of semitransitive consciousness cannot apprehend problems situated outside their sphere of biological necessity. Their interests center almost totally around survival, and they lack a sense of life on a more historic plane. The concept of semiintransitivity does not signify the closure of a person within himself, crushed by an all-powerful time and space. Whatever his state, man is an open being. Rather, semiintransitive consciousness means that his sphere of perception is limited, that he is impermeable to challenges situated outside the sphere of biological necessity. In this sense only, semiintransitivity represents a near disengagement between men and their existence. In this state, discernment is difficult. Men confuse their perceptions of the objects and challenges of the environment, and fall prey to magical explanations because they cannot apprehend true causality.
>
> As men amplify their power to perceive and respond to suggestions and questions arising in their context, and increase their capacity to enter into dialogue, not only with other men but with their world, they become "transitive." . . . Transitivity of consciousness makes man "permeable." It leads him to replace his disengagement from existence with almost total engagement.

Freire, *Education*, p. 17.

[53] Again, Paulo Freire gives an apt description of this condition.

> Perhaps the greatest tragedy of modern man is his domination by the force of these myths and his manipulation by organized advertising, ideological or otherwise. Gradually, without even realizing the loss, he relinquishes his capacity for choice; he is expelled from the orbit of decisions. Ordinary men do not perceive the tasks of the time; the latter are interpreted by an "elite" and presented in the form of recipes, of prescriptions, they drown in leveling anonymity, without hope and without faith, domesticated and adjusted.

Ibid., pp. 6–7.

[54] This issue is central in Rahner's anthropology, and he treats it in many places. See Karl Rahner, "Freedom," in Rahner et al., *Sacramentum Mundi*

II (N.Y.: Herder and Herder, 1968), pp. 361–362; also, K. Rahner, *Foundations of Christian Faith* (N.Y.: Seabury Press, 1978), pp. 93–104.

[55] Over the past several years, there have been several critiques of this system. To deal with them all would require a separate lengthy article. However, two recent critiques giving important background to anyone wishing to understand better the problems created for young people by the school are: James J. Coleman ed., *Youth: Transition to Adulthood* and John H. Martin, ed., *The Education of Adolescents* (Washington: U.S. Government Printing Office, 1976).

[56] I realize that such a "legitimizing of oppression" is entirely unconscious in youth ministry; and yet, for that matter, as unconscious it is all the more dangerous.

[57] Required reading for any youth ministry preparation program should be the fine statement by Gregory Baum in "Critical Theology," Chapter 9 of Gregory Baum, *Religion and Alienation* (N.Y.: Paulist Press, 1975), pp. 193–226.

[58] See the fine overview of these developments in Maria Harris, *Portrait of Youth Ministry* (New York: Paulist Press, 1981).

[59] We cannot be naive about the complications this striving will create for ourselves. Those who unveil oppressive structures will probably be labeled troublemakers and seen as "the enemy." Jürgen Moltmann put the matter as follows:

> . . . there is no solidarity with the victims of racism, sexism and capitalism without the betrayal of their betrayers. Whoever wants genuine communion with the victims must become the enemy of their enemies. Thus if he or she comes from the ranks of the enemy, he or she will become a betrayer. To become free from the oppressive prison of one's society means to become a "stranger among one's own people." Yet it is only through this estrangement that one can show to the oppressors the homeland of humanity. Whoever in a racist society, whoever in a patriarchal culture, whoever in a capitalistic economy betrays his or her "own world" for the sake of the victims witnesses to the love of God, lives in discipleship to Christ, spreads abroad hope and works for life against death.

Jürgen Moltmann with M. Douglas Meeks, "The Liberation of Oppressors," *Christianity and Crisis* (Dec. 25, 1978), p. 316.

[60] A seminal article is, John B. Metz, "Religion and Society in the Light of a Political Theology," *Harvard Theological Review* 61:4 (1968), pp. 507–523.

[61] Bernard Lonergan, *Method in Theology* (N.Y.: The Seabury Press, 1979), p. 238.

[62] Scott Hope, "The Writing Problem." Newsletter of The San Francisco Young Adult Network (944 Market St., San Francisco, CA 94102, Jan. 1978), pp. 2–3.

⁶³ Peter Marin, "The New Narcissism." *Harper's*, (Oct., 1975), p. 48.

⁶⁴ Marjorie Moffat, "Evangelization: A New Look at the Unchurched." *Living Light* 16:1 (1979), pp. 7–11.

⁶⁵ Karl Rahner, *The Christian Commitment: Essays in Pastoral Theology* (N.Y.: Sheed and Ward, 1963), p. 93.

⁶⁶ Ibid., pp. 99–100.

⁶⁷ Moltmann writes, "So in practice man is the greatest puzzle that man has. He needs to know himself, in order to live and to make himself recognizable to other people. But at the same time he must remain concealed from himself in order to be able to remain alive and free. For if he ever finally got 'behind himself,' and could establish what was the matter with him, nothing would any longer be the matter with him, but everything would be fixed and tied down, and he would be finished. The solution of the puzzle what man is would then at the same time be the final release from being human. As we experience being human, we experience it as a question, as freedom and as openness. 'We are, but we do not possess ourselves'—this is clearly the human condition. From this it follows that 'this is what we exist for in the first place.' " Jurgen Moltmann, *Man* (Philadelphia: Fortress Press, 1974), p. 2.

⁶⁸ "Life structure" is a concept treated extensively by Daniel Levinson.

> By "life structure" we mean the underlying pattern or design of a person's life at a given time. Here we are studying the lives of men. A man's life has many components: his occupation, his love relationship, his marriage and family, his relation to himself, his use of solitude, his roles in various social contexts—all the relationships with individuals, groups, and institutions that have significance for him. His personality influences and is influenced by his involvement in each of them. . . .
>
> The concept of life structure—the basic pattern or design of a person's life at a given time—gives us a way of looking at the engagement of the individual in society. It requires us to consider both self and the world, and the relationships between them. . . .
>
> How shall we go about describing and analyzing the life structure? The most useful starting point, I believe, is to consider the choices a person makes and how he deals with their consequences. The important choices in adult life have to do with work, family, friendships, and love relationships of various kinds, where to live, leisure, involvement in religious, political and community life, immediate and long-term goals.

Daniel Levinson, *The Seasons of a Man's Life* (N.Y.: Alfred A. Knopf, 1978), pp. 41–42.

⁶⁹ Aidan Kavanagh points out that to a large extent the way we communicate social values is through ritual. Ritual "carries" values in a

culture and keeps these values alive. To disrupt the rituals of a society is to break this chain of communicating values. The same point can be transposed to ritual-at-a-personal-level, which is what I mean by life-style or the pattern of one's actual living. These patterns embody values quite independently of whether or not one worships and of where or when one worships. See Aidan Kavanagh, "Teaching Through the Liturgy," *Notre Dame Journal of Education* 5:1 (1974), pp. 35–47.

⁷⁰ Ronald Blythe, *The View in Winter* (N.Y.: Harcourt Brace Jovanovich, 1979), p. 23.

⁷¹ Freedom in the United States too often reduces to a consumer's freedom: to use Crest rather than Ipana; to take Social Science 108 instead of Political Science 202; to work for J & L instead of for LTV; to drive a Malibu rather than a Mustang; to live in Rosewood rather than in Rosemont. Americans have external freedoms, but these are not the freedoms of self-transcendence. The freedom which makes men wonder about their own identity is that which shakes their identity to its core, terrifies them, makes demands on them, draws them into the pit of nothingness in order to confront them: "Now choose." For many, the first philosophical problem is that of suicide. Why do anything at all? Why live? Freedom is creation out of nothingness: an act of self-affirmation, for no particular reason, out of no necessity "because I *want* to." It is in exercising such freedom, brooding over an inner chaos, that man acts in the image of God spoken in the myth of Genesis.

Most of our young people, however, grow up in a totally man-made environment, designed to be as secure for them as possible, and to eliminate hunger, passion, chaos, ignorance, disease, conflict, despair.

Michael Novak, "The Unawareness of God," in Whalen, Ed., *The God Experience* (N.Y.: Newman, 1971), pp. 8–9.

⁷² Erik H. Erikson, "Reflections on Dr. Borg's Life Cycle," *Daedalus* 105:2 (Spring 1976), p. 5.

⁷³ Erikson, with his characteristic nuance, points out the many variables affecting this process. For instance, he writes,

[Identity] is dependent on the *past* for the resource of strong identifications made in childhood, while it relies on new models encountered in youth, and depends for its conclusion on workable roles offered in young adulthood. In fact, each subsequent stage of adulthood must contribute to its preservation and renewal.

The "socio" part of identity, then, must be accounted for in that communality within which an individual finds himself. No ego is an island unto itself. Throughout life the establishment and maintenance of that strength which can reconcile discontinuities and ambiguities depends on the support of parental as well as communal models. For youth depends on the ideological coherence of the world it is meant to take over, and therefore is sensitively aware of whether the system is strong enough in its traditional form to "confirm" and to be confirmed by the identity process, or so rigid or brittle as to suggest renovation, reformation, or revolution. Psychosocial identity, then, also has a *psychohistorical* side, and suggests the study of how life histories are inextricably interwoven with history. The study of psychosocial identity, therefore, depends on three complementarities—or are they three aspects of one complementarity?—namely, the personal coherence (the individual and role integration in his group), his guiding images and the ideologies of his time; his life history—and the historical moment.

Erik H. Erikson, *Life History and the Historical Moment* (N.Y.: W. W. Norton, 1975), p. 21.

[74] See Thomas McGowan, "The Unification Church," *The Ecumenist* 17:2 (Jan.–Feb. 1979), pp. 21–25.

[75] "Fidelity is the ability to sustain loyalties freely pledged in spite of the inevitable contradictions and confusions of value systems. It is the cornerstone of identity. . . ." Erikson, ". . . Dr. Borg," p. 25.

[76] Gregory Baum explores this idea systematically and compellingly in *Religion and Alienation*, especially in Chapter 9, "Critical Theology." See Baum, *Religion and Alienation* (N.Y.: Paulist Press, 1975), pp. 193–226. Another fine statement by Baum on this same issue is: "Values and Society" *The Ecumenist* 17:2 (Jan.–Feb. 1979), pp. 25–31.

[77] In affirming my position here, I do not deny there is a systematic noncommitment possible and even not uncommon. Such a noncommitment is described by Michael Novak thus:

> To survive in America, it is necessary for most people to hang loose, to play it cool, to drift, to avoid premature commitment. Life in a technological society is so specialized that it picks young people up and, as it were, places them on iron rails from which it is difficult to escape. One is pushed hard in grammar school in order to get into a good high school in order to get into a good college in order to get into a good graduate school in order to get into a good corporation in order to get into a good suburb in order to get into a good casket. To defend themselves against the competitive narrowing down, against the iron rungs of success, many commit themselves only piecemeal. They don't live by a life-project but by the absence of projects. They hold themselves in reserve. They wait. There is a form of other-directedness which is constituted, not by picking up signals for one's own behavior from the behavior of others, but by waiting for things to happen, waiting for things to break, waiting for excitement from outside.

Novak, "Unawareness," pp. 23–24.

If the way of noncommitment is one danger, the way of haste and of panic in not being able to tolerate the gradualness of growth is another and a greater danger. Actually, a good deal of religious autobiography is intensely aware of incompleteness and gradualness. In his *Confessions*, for example, Augustine, from one point of view, shows disgust for his dallying, but from another, sees it as his way, his step-by-stepness toward God.

[78] A recent essay on sexuality by Rosemary Haughton puts transformation as a key issue for growth in sexuality. See Rosemary Haughton, "Towards a Christian Theology of Sexuality," *Cross Currents*, 28:3 (1978), pp. 288–298. See also her earlier, related treatment of transformation in encounter, chapter 2 of *The Transformation of Man* (Springfield, Ill.: Templegate, 1967), pp. 41–84.

[79] Possibly the best single statement about the flux of this period is still Kenneth Keniston's essay, "Youth as a New State of Life," in his *Youth and Dissent* (N.Y.: Harcourt Brace Jovanovich, 1971).

[80] American literature abounds in compelling images of this curse, but perhaps no one states the problem as succinctly as does Flannery O'Connor's Hazel Motes in *Wise Blood:* "Nobody with a good car needs to be justified."

[81] The key to spirituality—one's lived spirituality—is to be found in the images that dominate one's imagination because these are what dictate the way our time and money are used and what our overall priorities are. In other words behind every life structure are the images of what life is thought to be all about. In the following passage, Gregory Baum explains how such images function:

> Sociologists tell us . . . that public values have an enormous impact on people's private values. For a while people may nourish their ideals of life from a great religious tradition, but by participating in economic life, they acquire a new self-understanding, and even without realizing it, they are transformed in accordance with the public ideals of profit and competition. We become concerned with promoting our own career; we think of our own advantage; we regard other people, if they are not related to us, as competitors, remain aloof from them, even suspicious, and seek a life that involves us as little as possible with the community at large. We dream of a government that keeps society tidy, protects property and investments, and leaves us alone to live out our private life without disturbance, Apart from the work we do to make money and promote our career, we want to live a private existence, have a good time, enjoy our hobbies, escape suffering, and remain free of obligations. A lovely weekend at the summer house on the lake—this makes it all worthwhile. That's the life! "Values and Society," p. 27.

[82] Dorothy Day, "Poverty and Precarity," *The Catholic Worker*, 45:7 (Sept. 1979), p. 1.

[83] . . . Christians (and in general people whose vision of life is determined by sharing and cooperation) must become *critics of the present society* [emphasis Baum's]. To promote the illusion that personal piety and personal

conversion can interject Christian values into society blinds people to the inherent power of society over consciousness, to the extent that Christians preach personal conversion and hold out the hope for the extension of private values to the public order, they pull the wool over people's eyes and in this sense actually help perpetuate the system that generates egotism. The recommendation of virtue can be, under certain circumstances, the legitimation of an unjust social order. What Christian preaching must do instead is to make people critics of society. Baum, "Values and Society," pp. 27–28.

Suggestions for
Further Reading

(including works cited in the text)

Arrupe, Pedro, "Catechesis and Inculturation." *Lumen Vitae* 33:1 (1978), pp. 45–50.

Baum, Gregory, *Religion and Alienation* (N.Y.: Paulist Press, 1975).

_____, "Values and Society," *The Ecumenist* 17:2 (Jan.-Feb. 1979).

Blythe, Ronald, *The View in Winter* (N.Y.: Harcourt Brace Jovanovich, 1979).

Coleman, James, ed., *Youth: Transition to Adulthood* (Chicago: University of Chicago Press, 1974).

Cooney, Nancy Hennessy, "Deciding for Yourself, Not by Yourself: A Christian Sex Education Program for Junior High Youth and Their Parents." *PACE* 6 (1975), Issues, Section G.

_____, *Sex, Sexuality and You* (Dubuque: W. C. Brown, 1980).

Coughlin, Kevin, "Motivating Adults for Religious Education." *The Living Light* 13:2 (1976), pp. 269–298.

Davis, Charles, "Religion and the Sense of the Sacred." *Catholic Theological Society of America Proceedings* 31 (1976), pp. 87–105.

Day, Dorothy, "Poverty and Precarity." *The Catholic Worker* 45:7 (Sept. 1979), p. 1.

Durka, Gloria and Joanmarie Smith, *Emerging Issues in Religious Education* (N.Y.: Paulist, 1976).

Erikson, Erik H., "Reflections on Dr. Borg's Life Cycle." *Daedalus* 105:2 (Spring 1976).

_____, *Life History and the Historical Moment* (N.Y.: W. W. Norton, 1975).

Evans, Donald, *Struggle and Fulfillment* (N.Y.: Collins, 1979).

Freire, Paulo, *Education for Critical Consciousness* (N.Y.: Seabury Press, 1973).

146

Goodman, Ellen, "What They're Selling, Parents Aren't Buying." *Washington Post* (Oct. 14, 1980).

Harris, Lis, "Persons in Need of Supervision." *The New Yorker* (Aug. 14, 1978), pp. 55–89.

Haughton, Rosemary, *The Transformation of Man* (Springfield, IL: Templegate, 1967).

———, "Towards a Christian Theology of Sexuality." *Cross Currents* 28:3 (1978), pp. 288–298.

Kavanagh, Aidan, "Teaching through the Liturgy." *Notre Dame Journal of Education* 5:1 (1974), pp. 35–47.

Kenniston, Kenneth, *Youth and Dissent* (N.Y.: Harcourt Brace Jovanovich, 1971).

Kett, Joseph F., *Rites of Passage: Adolescence in America, 1790 to the Present*, (N.Y.: Basic Books, 1977).

Konopka, Gisela, *The Adolescent Girl in Conflict* (Englewood Cliffs, NJ: Prentice-Hall, 1966).

———, *Young Girls: A Portrait of Adolescence* (Englewood Cliffs, NJ: Prentice-Hall, 1976).

Langer, Susanne K., *Philosophy in a New Key: A Study in The Symbolism of Reason. Rite and Art* (Cambridge, MA: Harvard University Press, 1957).

Levinson, Daniel, *The Seasons of a Man's Life* (N.Y.: Alfred A. Knopf, 1978).

Lonergan, Bernard, *Method in Theology* (N.Y.: The Seabury Press, 1979).

———, *Collection* (N.Y.: Herder & Herder, 1967).

———, *A Second Collection* (Philadelphia: Westminster Press, 1974).

Lynch, William F., *Images of Faith: An Exploration of the Ironic Imagination* (Notre Dame, IN: Univ. of Notre Dame Press, 1973).

Marthaler, Berard L., *Catechetics in Context* (Huntington, IN: Our Sunday Visitor Press, 1973).

———, and Marianne Sawicki, eds., *Catechesis: Realities and Visions* (Washington: U.S. Catholic Conference, 1977).

Martin, John H., ed., *The Education of Adolescents* (Washington: U.S. Government Printing Office, 1976).

Metz, John B., "Religion and Society in the Light of a Political Theology." *Harvard Theological Review* 61:4 (1968), pp. 507–523.

Moltmann, Jurgen, *Man* (Philadelphia: Fortress Press, 1974).

National Inventory of Parish Catechetical Programs, A. (Washington: U.S. Catholic Conference, 1978).

Nelson, C. Ellis, *Where Faith Begins* (Atlanta: John Knox Press, 1967).

Piveteau, Didier, and James Dillon, "Two Scholarly Views on Religious Education: Lee and Westerhoff." *Lumen Vitae* 32:1 (1977), pp. 7–44.

Rahner, Karl, *Theological Investigations*, vol. 7, 8 (N.Y.: Herder & Herder, 1971), vol. 9 (1972).

_____, *Foundations of Christian Faith* (N.Y.: Seabury Press, 1978).

Robinson, James M., ed., *Religion and the Humanizing of Man* (Waterloo, Ont.: Council on the Study of Religion, 1972).

Steinfels, Margaret O'Brien, "Beyond the Medical Solution." *Commonweal* (May 23, 1980), pp. 310–312.

Strommen, Merton, *Bridging the Gap* (Minneapolis: Augsburg, 1973).

_____, *Five Cries of Youth* (N.Y.: Harper & Row, 1974).

Tobin, William, ed., *International Catechetical Congress: Selected Documentation* (Washington: U.S. Catholic Conference, 1972).

Upton, Julia Ann, "A Solution to the Infant Baptism Problem." *The Living Light* 16:4 (1979), pp. 484–496.

"Vision of Youth Ministry, A." (Washington: U.S. Catholic Conference, 1976).

Warren, Michael, "Evangelization: A Catechetical Concern." *The Living Light* 10:4 (1973), pp. 487–496.

_____, *A Future for Youth Catechesis* (N.Y.: Paulist, 1975).

_____, ed., *Youth Ministry: A Book of Readings* (N.Y.: Paulist, 1977).

_____, ed., *Resources for Youth Ministry* (N.Y.: Paulist, 1978).

Westerhoff, John, "A Call to Catechesis." *The Living Light* 14:3 (1977), pp. 354–358.

Whalen, Joseph P., ed., *The God Experience* (N.Y.: Newman, 1971).